ht

THE WORLD ACCORDING TO
nickferrari

THE WORLD ACCORDING TO
nickferrari

He's funny, he's outrageous – you'll love him!

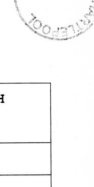

NICK FERRARI

To those who love or support me...
you unfortunate souls know who you are!

Published by John Blake Publishing Ltd,
3 Bramber Court, 2 Bramber Road,
London W14 9PB, England

www.blake.co.uk

First published in hardback in 2006

ISBN 1 84454 241 6

British Library Cataloguing-in-Publication Data:

A catalogue record for this book is available from the British Library.

Design by www.envydesign.co.uk

Printed in Great Britain by Creative Print & Design, Wales.

1 3 5 7 9 10 8 6 4 2

Illustrations by Mike Mosedale

Papers used by John Blake Publishing are natural, recyclable products
made from wood grown in sustainable forests. The manufacturing
processes conform to the environmental regulations
of the country of origin.

Contents

Brits in the air? Fine, so long as they're called Stephanie...   1

Guess what, Son — I'm a chair!   7

How Mogadishu taught me to stop worrying and love my dentist   15

I don't hate cyclists, I just want to protect their knackers   21

The rise and rise of Billy No Mates   27

Why I make foxes laugh and Wayne Rooney stare   37

Why should I love my bum? Nobody else does...   45

Myrtle the Fresian: pin-up for the discerning heavy metal fan?   55

Goat dung: the new black   61

Why the Royal Family really should be a laughing matter...   69

Technology? I'd rather go down the Dog and Duck   83

Why I feel like Kate Moss in the flyovers...   95

Porridge all round, and pass the apple sauce 105

Make poverty history? I'd rather make Bono history . . . 113

Witchdoctors: alive and well and living in Chancery Lane 121

In defence of Christmas 127

Why I'll take Clacton-on-Sea over St Tropez any time 135

Europe: nul points! 141

Vote Nick Ferrari for Archbishop if you want the F word in church 149

Prince Philip in suspenders? Now that's entertainment! 155

The laughing policemen 161

Requiem to a flying blackboard rubber 169

Having it all, and why you can't — even if you're Germaine Greer 175

A night out in London 183

Big Brother might be watching me, but I'm certainly
  not watching him . . . 191

America? China? Nah . . . it's all happening in Tescoland 197

Giving Auntie a kick up the jacksie 203

Help! Is there an aromatherapist in the house? 209

How do we put up with Ken? And how does he put up with me? 217

If in doubt, ask Sid 223

Gordon Ramsay: prick with a fork 229

London 2012? Let's have a Whopper and curly fries instead 235

The Spanish Inquisition: alive and well and living in Holmes Place   241

That's enough touchy-feely — let's bring back the nasty party   247

Dead cows and white elephants   257

Order, order! Why some honourable members need some real
   whipping into shape   263

Did you hear the one about The Pope and The Most Holy
   Carmelite Order of Prestatyn?   271

"It's a pretty unpolished airline these days."

Brits in the air? Fine, so long as they're called Stephanie...

Remember the days when air travel was the preserve of the glamorous, the jet set and the elite? Well, if you do, you just won't believe what it's like now. In the course of being a reporter for a series of national newspapers and shuttling across the Atlantic fairly regularly when I was working for Fox TV in the United States as part of Rupert Murdoch's organisation, I was exposed to just about every variety of air travel you can imagine.

One image will never leave me. To explain it fully, I need to put it in context. Whenever I crossed the Atlantic I always chose, whenever possible, Virgin Atlantic. Sir Richard Branson's airline is nothing short of genius. They consistently have the best facilities, the smartest crew and the most enjoyable flights (there – that should secure the next upgrade or three...). Because of the number of air miles I chalked up with Virgin Atlantic, I found myself upgraded to a gold-card holder and therefore able to enjoy lounge access at all airports. I was flying from Gatwick to Newark and, as I was a member of the Executive Club, I was able to wait until almost the last minute to board the aircraft – not only was a special announcement made in the first-class lounge, but a stunningly stylish young woman, complete with the Virgin Atlantic uniform hugging her in all the right places, arrived to escort me to the departure gate. We walked through and I was in the blissful mental state of being a mix between being James Bond and a leading captain of industry. Then, as I neared the boarding gates, I looked to my right and saw the last few members of economy class being boarded for the flight.

And there it was: Atlantic traveller, British style.

Dad had the body mass of a Sumo wrestler but the height of a National Hunt jockey. He was red-faced, sweating and wearing a T-shirt that strained at every seam. At first glance it appeared to have the Ford logo on the front of it; closer inspection revealed that it was not Ford that was spelled out on his ample chest but FCUK! Why would a grown man want to walk around with a slogan like that on his bosom?

Behind was his wife wearing a hideous white shell suit that immediately made you give thanks that smoking on all aircraft has now been banned – if anyone had dropped a match or anything slightly combustible near her, she would have gone up in flames in a second thanks to all the chemicals involved in the production of her hideous outfit. But the crowning lump of pooh in the overflow pipe was the teenage daughter dragging herself along sulkily some five yards behind her parents. This was a girl who had her hair pulled so tightly behind her face she was almost striking an oriental grimace; she had rings in both her ears, her nose and on most of her fingers, and one through her naval – I was only grateful that she was wearing faded tracksuit trousers on her bottom half to show that there wasn't one anywhere else. But the item that set off this ensemble to the best was her T-shirt. It was green with the following slogan in vivid letters: LAST NIGHT I F***ED THE DRUMMER! It made me wonder if there was anything people would not wear as a slogan on a T-shirt. What about a picture of a pile of steaming horse crap, or the slogan I'M A MORON, or a picture of two rats fighting over the remnants of a dead fox that's been mangled by the side of a motorway. Trouble is, I've probably given a few fashion designers some ideas there!

It just made me long for the glamorous days of air travel. It used to have an air of refinement and style – we're talking Sean Connery as James Bond touching down in Jamaica in *Dr No*, not 20,000 people stuck at Gatwick airport on a sweltering bank holiday waiting to get their flights to Spain or Greece but who have been stuck because of the latest dispute with French air traffic control. If you were to fetch back some of the frequent flyers from the fifties and walk them through today's departure lounges in Stansted, Birmingham and Gatwick, they would freeze with horror. They would see people feeding themselves with their hands, guzzling fizzy drinks, screaming at loutish children and then queuing – sometimes for hours – to be boarded on to planes and be seated in conditions similar to those that a sardine experiences in a tin. It is surely close to immoral the way some airlines treat their economy class passengers.

I am more than happy to pass on to you some of the pointers I have learned from the amount of air travel I enjoyed years ago. The first one echoes the words of Shakespeare: what's in a name? As you sit there, you need to hear a captain with the correct name introduce himself to your flight. You hear the bing bing of the in-flight announcement system and then, 'Good morning, ladies and gentlemen, this is your pilot speaking. My name is Captain Charles Smyth and welcome aboard this non-stop flight from London Heathrow to New York Kennedy Airport. We will be taxiing out to runway two in about ten minutes, once our luggage doors are fully fastened. Please sit back in your seats and enjoy our excellent onboard service.'

Compare that with the possibility of the following: 'Wotcher! My name's Wayne, and Big Dave's beside me here in the cockpit. We're gonna get out of here just as soon as we can, but we had a hell of a skinful last night and my head's not really clear until I take a couple more Nurofen. Those of you sitting in business class, why not check out Tracy – I've had her at least half a dozen times and she bangs like an outside toilet door in a gale.'

Or: 'My name is Abdul, I'm not prepared to tell you anything else – I just wish death and destruction on the hideous jackal sons of the infidel and the capitalist oppressive west.'

Once you're past the in-flight announcement from the pilot, the next thing to listen out for is the names of the air hostesses. Those of you reading this or who are just about to or have just had daughters, if in any way you think they might one day be involved in air travel, here's a hint: the names they get will mark them for life. Certain girls' names are meant for first class, others for business – and many others, I am afraid, are decidedly for the back of the bus. For example, in first class you have the Stephanies, Sofias, Jessicas, Philippas, Hannahs and Rebeccas; Sarah, Becky and Jenny will get you into business class; and at the back of the bus, I am afraid to say, there will always be the Sharons, the Tracys and the Alices.

Guess what, Son — I'm a chair!

This is how it works on the radio. You set up a story, and then you line up an interview. 'The price of fish has gone up this week by 500 per cent, and this means that nobody can afford to buy a nice bit of halibut for their supper. Here to talk about it is the spokesman for the British Fish Board, Arthur Cod.'

So far, so good. But the way things are going, this is how the conversation is likely to progress:

'Actually, Nick, it's spokesperson.'

'Pardon?'

'I'm the spokes*person* for the British Fish Board. Not the spokes*man*.'

'Why? Aren't you a man?

'Yes, I am a man, but that's not the point.'

'What is the point?'

'I think it's derogatory.'

'No, it's de-radio, actually.'

And we end up not having a conversation about the price of fish, but what word I should use to describe this bloke.

A case in point is the use of the word 'coloured'. To the innocent among us it was just a word used to describe non-white people and there was no suggestion of it hiding any insult or bad meaning. My generation, and perhaps the one above, then grew up in a very different kind of Britain – multi-coloured, multi-ethnic, multi-cultured – and it was suddenly decided that we shouldn't say 'coloured'. Black was black, white was white, and suddenly the word seemed to have some slightly unpleasant undercurrent. Now the pendulum seems to be switching again: I recently had Trevor Philips, head of the Commission for Racial Equality, on the show. He told me he had been addressing a Muslim Conservative association at the Conservative Party Conference, and that he had explained to them that he felt that there perhaps, after all, a place for the word 'coloured'. So now we're all bloody confused about what we can and can't say. Of course we don't want to offend anybody, but we don't know how to go about not offending them.

At seven o'clock in the morning, most of London is just getting up (although some of London is just getting home). People should be lying in bed, scratching themselves as they wake up slowly and wonder what the day has in store for them. They should be grappling with issues no more serious than whether they fancy Shreddies or Weetabix, or whether or not they want jam on their toast. Or honey, perhaps. So what makes them pick up the phone at such an ungodly hour and call a radio station like mine? What are the subjects that make them forget their Crunchy Nut Cornflakes and sit up and listen – and sometimes speak – instead?

This is the one subject that is always bound to get the switchboard lights flashing: race and religion, and what is offensive and what is not. My chats with ordinary Londoners from all sorts of cultural backgrounds are, for me, a masterclass in what it is acceptable to say, where sensibilities lie and what people find to be offensive. And I have come to the conclusion that there is a white, middle-class, liberal, *Guardian*-reading chatterati so hell-bent on perceiving slights and insults where none exist that not only do they risk turning our country into a humourless, bland place to be, they are doing serious harm to the very people they think they are, in some perverse way, protecting; and in so doing they are denuding our very language.

On the same show that Trevor Philips appeared on, I took a call from a man in Walthamstow. 'I'm sick of all this political correctness, Nick,' he tells me. 'Look, I'm a black bloke. I just want to get on and live my life. You can call me coloured if you want, just so long as you don't do it in an offensive way. Or you can call me black, I don't care.' Then he gave me an example of what he has to put up with. 'I took some time off work recently. When I got back, I went into a meeting and my boss said, 'Ah, Gary, good to see you back.'

'As a joke, I replied, "What do you mean, it's good to see that I'm black? I've always been black. How dare you say that!"

'My boss freezes with absolute terror. "I didn't say that." He turns to someone next to him.

"You noticed that I said back, not black, didn't you? I want it written down in a report."'

So far, so Ricky Gervais. In Gary's case, this fear of seeing offence where there is none meant that he couldn't even make a little joke at his own expense. But it can have even more ridiculous outcomes. When workers at a certain West Midlands borough council were sent novelty stress-relievers in the shape of a pig, they ended up being banned on the basis that they 'offended' one woman who worked there. The toys just happened, by unfortunate coincidence, to be delivered around the beginning of Ramadan: this Muslim employee went to her boss and told him she didn't think it was right that they had toy pigs. The pig, she said, was not a toy in the Muslim religion.

So the council had two options:

1. They could go completely bloody mad and ban all pig products in the office. Or,
2. They could take the employee aside and say, 'Look, there's honestly no offence intended. These are just little pig toys. Obviously you don't want one, and we quite understand that, but ultimately what can we say? That we mustn't

have cows advertising milk because it's offensive to Hindus?'

Of course, there are no prizes for guessing which way it went. All the toys were banned, calendars in the office that depicted pigs were banned, one person even had a tissue-box cover with Winnie the Pooh on it – that was banned too. The whole office was excised of anything to do with pigs.

The upshot of this is that it sets the cause for integration for ordinary Muslims back about twenty years. Why? Because there is bound to be a vicious, evil, nasty, pernicious group of white Brits who see what has happened and say, 'There you are, those Muslims are at it again.' Only of course it's not the Muslims at it again – it's one woman finding offence where there is none.

Some people just wake up in the morning *wanting* to be offended. (I have a sneaking suspicion that it's the same people who ride bicycles.) At best their complaints are just funny; at worst they put us under the jurisdiction of a kind of thought police who believe they are in a position to stop us from, as they see it, seeing no evil, hearing no evil and speaking no evil. As a result of the machinations of these people, two advertisements were recently taken off the air that perfectly demonstrate the ridiculous situation we now find ourselves in.

The first was for KFC. The advert depicted a bunch of people singing a song while they munched their chicken and rejoiced about the value they were getting for a couple of quid. The advert was withdrawn because people considered that it encouraged children to have bad manners. What a dereliction of duty on behalf of the parents! It's *their* job to teach children not to speak with their mouths full, not the television's. The reason I'm the size I am is because I like the occasional glass of wine. This is not the fault of Oddbins – it's something I take personal responsibility for myself.

The second advert was for the Renault Megane. It featured the tune 'I See You Baby Shaking That Ass', and it showed people dancing and shaking. This, it seems, offended people for two reasons. Firstly they were upset that it showed – and before you read the next word please look away if you are of a sensitive nature – bottoms (albeit fully clothed ones). Secondly, it was deemed to be offensive to sufferers of

Parkinson's disease. Now I have nothing but sympathy for the sufferers of Parkinson's – my late grandfather was afflicted by it, and I know how terrible it can be. But do these people honestly think a bunch of executives in the ad agency came up with this idea and said, 'It'll sell lots of cars. Oh, and we can offend Parkinson's sufferers into the deal as well.' I think not...

So now we don't have fat people, we have people with an enlarged physical condition; we don't have foreign food, we have ethnic cuisine; we don't have sex changes, we have gender reassignments. We have to be careful about blackmailing people, or writing on a blackboard. And we most certainly cannot refer to a chairman, or even a chairwoman. It's even making us lose the respect of our kids.

'What happened at work today, Dad?'

'I had a fantastic day today, son.'

'Really, what happened?'

'I got a big promotion.'

'That *is* fantastic, Dad. What are you now?'

'I'm a chair.'

'A chair?'

'That's right son. A chair.'

'Er ... great, Dad. Nice one.'

How Mogadishu taught me to stop worrying and love my dentist

It all started because I had my nose to the stumps.

Perhaps I should explain a little further. In the early 1970s, at the tender age of eleven, I was a member of the worst school cricket team in all of north-west Kent – and that's really saying something. Our fielding was on the wrong side of dreadful, but it was incomparably brilliant when compared to our batting, which we simply couldn't do to save our lives. We certainly had no chance of winning a game by dazzling our opponents with our brilliant innings, and so our only hope of success lay in getting the other team out for even fewer runs than our paltry, embarrassing total.

We had – now how can I put this – a fairly strong-minded teacher. In fact, he made Sir Alex Ferguson look like a happy-go-lucky, laid-back, West-coast hippy of a guy. He insisted that I, as wicketkeeper, should crouch literally with my nose against the wickets so that I was on hand for any stumping opportunities that presented themselves if the ball got so much as nicked by the bat. Now this is fine if your opponent is of the more docile and gentle persuasion – a nice slow ball that is likely to bounce anywhere but in the direction of the wicketkeeper; but our bowlers were more in the Freddie Flintoff mould without the talent – long, straight and fast – in which case it was suicidal madness to stand where I was told to put myself. It was really only a matter of time…

I felt sure I had the ball covered. I saw it bounce on the dry pitch. I raised my gloves to make a perfect catch, which is when the full force of my incompetence kicked in: the ball smacked into my mouth, I fell to the ground, and when I come up for air I'm spitting blood and, more crucially, about half my teeth.

So began years and years of painful dentistry.

Did I say painful? I mean excruciating torment. Not for me the urbane little trips to the surgery where the worst you had to put up with was that copy of *Country Life* from 1965 and daft questions about where you're going on holiday when you've got your mouth packed full of scaffolding. That, to me, would have been a walk in the park – well, maybe a slightly strenuous jog in the park, but you get my drift. And back in the bad old days, dentists weren't anything like as advanced in terms of drugs and techniques as they are now – going to the dentists was a matter of good, old-fashioned horror. You knew how badly it was going to hurt by how much the dentist denied it was going to. 'You won't feel this injection a bit,' they would lie, seconds before sticking a two-foot needle into your gums that felt like it was spearing through your eyeball and into your brain. Gradually I became conditioned to react to these monsters with nothing less than total, blinding fear. At great expense, I had to have an anaesthetist standing by for the simplest operations so that I could be put to sleep and forget my fear. A simple filling, for me, turned into a scene from *Holby City*.

Back in the dark days of dentistry, ensuring good colour matches of teeth was a hit-and-miss affair, which is why you will never find a picture of Nick Ferrari between the ages of eleven and thirty flashing a toothy grin.

And so, when I was offered a freebie session of teeth-whitening by a dentist who was running a promotion on the radio show, I understandably declined – too scared, you see. It was only when he offered to inject himself with anything he wanted to stick into my gums that I started to have a slightly different view of dentists. Perhaps, after all, they weren't the psychotic nutters hell-bent on inflicting as much pain on me as possible that I thought they were. And it's not that I have a sadistic streak, but there was something incredibly comforting about watching this chap stick a needle in his gums – so much so that I didn't feel a thing as he did the same to me.

As I relaxed in the chair for what I knew was going to be a good long stint, I was handed a pair of high-tech, space-age goggles through which I could watch movies. Having seen how the potential discomfort of others had soothed my fearful soul, I decided that I would be best to choose a movie that depicted violence, pain and the suffering of other people. *Black Hawk Down*, I decided, was the vehicle for me: whatever dental discomfort I was to go through, it couldn't be as bad as those poor marines chasing through the war-ravaged streets of Mogadishu.

It worked a treat! I came out with a splendid set of pearly whites and a much improved mental attitude towards my friends the dentists...

"On second thoughts… Can I just take a pair of cycle clips?"

I don't hate cyclists, I just want to protect their knackers

Let's get one thing absolutely straight about the congestion tax (or 'charge' as some people like to call it). It is absolutely, bona fide, fundamentally, one hundred per cent wrong. We're supposed to have a socialist mayor, but frankly you could well imagine Attila the Hun wreaking horrible violence on his top transport man for suggesting such a measure, on the basis that it might make him appear a little too far to the right.

Here's the lunacy of it. For the captains of industry, the people who make all the money, eight quid is small change – they throw it in and don't even notice it; and it doesn't really matter to them anyway because their companies will probably assume the charge. The same goes for those city whiz kids racing around in their Porsches from one champagne bar to another – they probably spend more than that on their Double Decaff Skinny Macchiato with a Twist every morning, and just don't feel the pain. The people it affects are the firefighters, and the office cleaners, and the people who have to take their kids to school – all of a sudden it's them who have to find this money they can hardly afford. How can that be a socialist policy, or one that is acceptable to a socialist mayor? We try to persuade these key workers to come and live in the city, but the moment they get in their car, we hit them with this.

So what are the options if you don't want to pay congestion tax? Don't tell me public transport is OK – it's an absolute disaster. You try to catch a bus: it won't turn up on time; if you're very, *very*, lucky you'll get a seat, but you'll probably sit next to some crackhead dope-dealer who is almost certainly going to want to rip you to shreds or try to sell you drugs, and you'll be lucky to get away with your life. Or you try to catch a train: the windows have all been etched by those kids who carve into the glass with special knives; and the seats are dirty at the best, ripped to shreds at the worst; and let's face it, you *are* going to be the person that the mumbling nutter nursing his can of lager decides to come and sit next to. The only time to travel by train is a brief window between 10.30 in the morning (when the office workers are at work) and 2.30 in the afternoon (when the winos wake up); any time other than that and it is absolute Hades. I am utterly convinced that if you tried to transport livestock in those sort of conditions, you'd have the animal-rights activists firebombing your house and eco-warriors living up the trees in your garden. Do you remember the advertising campaign one of the train companies came up with a while back, boasting about the fact that each day they shift more people than took part in the D-Day landings? Why would you think this is a good thing? People *died* in the D-Day landings. Horribly.

The bottom line is this: people love their cars. And they cost us a lot of money: we spend more on buying them than anyone else in Europe because of all the taxes; we have the most expensive petrol, the most expensive road tax and the most expensive insurance. We're funding the government on four or five different levels, and then they have the brass neck to say, 'Oh, by the way, if you want to drive in the city, it's an extra eight quid.'

Now obviously I'm not saying that London's roads do not have a deep-seated traffic problem. Indeed, it is ripping into the very fabric of society as we know it, as is illustrated by Nick Ferrari's Law of Lateness. This states that the deeper the friction in your relationship, the more traffic you'll be stuck in or the later the train will be. You've been promising for the last three weeks that you'll be home early tonight so that you can all go out for dinner together – a nice cosy evening with your well-adjusted nuclear family. Bugger me if that isn't the one time they decide to dig up the high street and put in a one-way system that takes you via Aldershot, or some silly sod has thrown himself under a train at Herne Hill and the whole network's down...

So something clearly needs to be done, but there's a simple solution to London's traffic problems: build more roads. Don't give me any of this green crap about everybody ditching their cars and getting on their bikes. Let's build a bloody big road right through the middle of Eltham like they wanted to a few years back, and take it right over the river – or even under the river. Let's have some intelligent thought processes. Let's do what they do in some American cities and make the bridges one way. And please, let's stop carving up more and more of our roads and giving them to cyclists! Not only is their ridiculous garb an obvious target for the fashion police, but those green cycle boxes by traffic lights are the final insult to us drivers. They are supposed to give cyclists a good head start, but if anyone can find a cyclist who can travel as quickly as my Mercedes, will somebody please send him an application form for the Tour de France at the double? I'm driving a car, for crying out loud! It's a fact of life: cars fast, bikes slow – you're going to have to get out of the way! The only purpose those green boxes serve is allowing me to choose which one of the buggers I'm going to terrorise when it's time for the off.

There's nothing worse than a smug cyclist telling you how fit they are and how quickly they got into work on their bike. Fine – at least I don't smell like a teenage boys' changing room when I arrive. And my desire to get cyclists off the road even had the support of the scientific community. It has now been conclusively shown that male cyclists who wear those ridiculous tight cycling shorts are far more likely to become impotent. They cut off the flow of blood to their genitals and it sends their potency plummeting. So you see, cyclists of London, it's not that we hate you – it's just that we're trying to protect your knackers. And if Ken Livingstone was to stop making life so hard for us drivers, we'd be free to continue our good work in peace.

The rise and rise of Billy No Mates

If it's true, as somebody once said, that a society gets the politicians that it deserves, what *on earth* have we done to get this lot?

It seems to me that the whole idea of politics is currently flawed. Each time an election of any sort rolls around – be it a general election, a local election, a European election or even an election to vote in the local librarian – politicians unite as one to urge the electorate to come out and vote. 'It's very important,' they tell us. 'It's your duty!'

What utter tosh!

It is sickening to think about the promises and pleas politicians make at each election. Just look at the election before last. A party was actually voted into power on the assurance that it would not introduce university top-up fees. A couple of years into their administration, it becomes necessary for all of their MPs to be 'whipped' into shape so that they can put through a policy that they had actually told the electorate they were not going to use.

And then they have the brass neck to tell us it is important that we vote!

If I had my way, I would do it very, very differently. It should not be my duty to have to vote for somebody I don't like. I currently live in a part of London where a donkey wearing a Labour rosette would be sure to be voted in. So I could waste my vote by going for the other parties, or just join in with the winners and see the donkey make its majestic progress into the House of Commons.

This is obviously wrong. So, welcome to General Election Nick Ferrari style.

As many parties as wanted to would be able to stand, but at the end of every single ballot paper would be one box that would simply say 'None of the Above'. This would allow people who are increasingly dissatisfied with the bunch of back-slapping, half-baked, useless cronies who give themselves and all their friends as many jobs as they can, to express their utter disgust.

And before any of you go getting any ideas, I hereby declare that *I* shall become leader of the None of the Above Party – you can consider this book to be my manifesto.

On a serious note, this would allow us to show that, while we *are* interested in politics, while we *do* care about the system that educates our children, runs our hospitals, looks after our elderly, tries to combat crime on the street and even takes the occasional look at the environment, we do *not* necessarily believe that the way it's currently put together is correct.

Whenever this conversation comes up on my radio programme, you will hear callers phoning in saying we should adopt the same system that they have in Australia – the system in which voters are actually fined if they refuse to vote at the general election. This is simply wrong. It means that people will be forced to vote for a party or a politician in which they have no trust, belief or interest.

Let me make the first of many confessions. I have deliberately scribbled across my ballot paper in a recent election of one sort or another. I did it in an attempt to make the point that I had no confidence in the sort of people who were available to be voted for. However, it will go down as a 'spoiled vote'. This makes me sound as if I have the mental capabilities of an elderly, retarded flea, or that I was actually a member of the care in the community project who had been allowed out for the day. In fact, I was wholly aware of what I was doing but had no way to vent my frustration and anger within the fairly rigid constraints of the voting system. Hence my belief in the None of the Above system.

In the past I have been quite interested by politics, and in my late teens I actually actively canvassed for one party during a general election. Now, before any senior representatives of any of the major parties start scrambling through their archives in the desperate fear that they will uncover that Nick Ferrari actually worked on their behalf in the late seventies or early eighties, I hasten to add that I will not be revealing my allegiances – and it's not who you'd think! But what it gave me was an insight into the system: the most important consideration for this particular party was not whether they had the best man or woman for the job, nor whether their leader had made the best impression in all the television broadcasts, nor even whether we had the right policies; it was how many people I could fit into my car to drive to the polling booths if it was a rainy day. As I was at that time driving a Morris 1100, I was viewed with little regard as it would appear I would be hard-pushed to get more than three old ducks in at any one time. When I volunteered to round up people and drive them to the vote polling booths – even against their will, but with the promise of a lift home and a bottle of Sanatogen for their trouble – it didn't seem to cut any ice. My career as a political activists came to a rapid end, but I remember it vividly: the *West Wing* it wasn't.

There are many puzzling things about the world of politics, and one of the great conundrums is how the successful exponents of the dark art manage to do so well. For instance, let's invent a phoney politician for a phoney party: we will call him Billy No Mates of the Sensible Party. Billy went to a grammar school and then on to a decent university where he studied Hebrew and Sanskrit and came out with a 2.1. Then, having wasted all of his sixth form and university education on bizarre subjects, he realised his true vocation lay in politics. Because of the system we currently employ, this is no problem for Billy. He simply writes scores of letters to MPs from as many political parties as he can think of, saying that he has a deep-seated and long-held interest in politics (it actually surfaced about eight weeks ago at a cider-and-gin party in a squat in Battersea) and he would be willing to work untold hours for very little pay, if any, as a researcher for one of the MPs. Billy then sits back and waits for the letters to come back. Eventually somebody cracks and Billy gets a job as a researcher for the third undersecretary of the Welsh Lamb Marketing Ministry. There, through a combination of shameless brown-nosing and occasional hard work, he shines. And enjoying the patronage of the Minister of Welsh Lamb production, he eventually gets given the chance to run as an MP on his own.

Fast-forward the tape some ten years. Billy No Mates, an MP with the Sensible Party, is now in politics and desperate to climb the greasy poll. What does he do? He slavishly follows all party directions, tells any waiting journalist or TV or radio crew that his leader is an absolute genius (while secretly plotting with other party bigwigs to bring the oaf down) and says that he realises he is there just for the benefit of his constituents.

He occasionally attends ceremonies in his own constituency but finds them desperately boring. Eventually, a bit of fame starts to beckon and they come looking for Billy for a junior role in one of the ministries. Fairly quickly, Billy No Mates ascends to the role of Agriculture Secretary in the government run by the Sensible Party. Billy knows nothing about agriculture. He was raised in a flat above a video shop and off licence just next to a council estate in Corby. The nearest he has ever been to agriculture was to buy a packet of bacon or six eggs from the local Co-Op.

He does well in that job. He agrees that his party leader, otherwise known as the Prime Minister, is an utter genius, and never says anything against the party line. His long-standing affair with his secretary is never discovered. As a consequence, at the next reshuffle he is promoted to Northern Ireland Secretary. Billy has never been to Northern Ireland in his life. If you were to say sectarian troubles to him, he would probably think it was a punk rock band from the late seventies. He thinks the Orange Men are probably a children's cartoon series and Bloody Sunday is when you're stuck at home with a car to wash and the kids are playing up. But that doesn't matter, because Billy is now in charge of the brief for Northern Ireland. So he has gone from knowing nothing about agriculture to running the government department about it and now the same as happened with Northern Ireland.

In the very tricky position of Northern Ireland Secretary, Billy is an instant success. Fortunately there are no bombs and very few people shoot each other – so there's another promotion in the next reshuffle. Billy is now Foreign Secretary!

Back at school, Billy's grades in geography always hovered around a D – except for his GCSEs when he actually managed to score an E. To Billy, Rio Grande is a football player and the Yangtze is a rather embarrassing condition you don't talk about at dinner parties. G8 is just another pop group and the Oslo Accord is available in both hatchback and coupé with air conditioning and leather upholstery.

You probably know where I am going to have this story end. Billy is such a blinding success in the role of Foreign Secretary that, when the Sensible Party has a ruthless back-stabbing shakedown of their leadership and a new man is needed to become Prime Minster, Billy 'Safe Hands' No Mates is there. We have a Prime Minster who has come through a series of jobs for which he has no ability, talent or training but who has simply kept his nose clean. He now stands in control of this country, despite never having done an actual day's work in his life.

And that last fact seems to be true of many of our leading politicians today! How can that be right? How is it that they can be in a position where they believe they are so intellectually able and so philanthropically versatile that we should fund every aspect of their lifestyle? My solution is this: every now and again, however senior the politician, they should be forced to start up a business or go out and work for a month or two in a proper job. Then, the next time you see them standing up in the Houses of Parliament, fighting with each other or telling us how we have got to tighten our belts, be more prudent or take pension advice, at least they will have seen the real world.

"Oh, bloody well bagged man...! That makes three of the buggers this morning."

Why I make foxes laugh and Wayne Rooney stare

I shot a fox when I was small, and it was the right thing to do.

Foxes, you see, are not the cute little beasties they're made out to be in Beatrix Potter books. They are not cuddly animals with wet noses and bright eyes. They are as vicious as Joe Pesci in *Goodfellas* and as calculating as Peter Mandelson. Well, perhaps not quite that calculating, but certainly pretty shrewd.

To be fair, I'm hardly the Judge Dredd of foxes. I've only ever killed one, and that was thirty years ago. I was brought up on a smallholding in Kent. It was more of a hobby for my parents than a serious concern, but we had all sorts of animals there: donkeys, sheep, ponies and, of course, chickens. So obviously we were a prime target for the conniving foxes – they would kill and steal the chickens, and even attack young lambs. A two-day-old lamb doesn't stand a chance against a wily old fox.

Now the trouble with foxes attacking your chickens is not that you lose the occasional chicken. The problem is that you lose *all* your chickens: foxes have no discriminatory powers, and once you've got one in your henhouse, it's going to be carnage. He won't just kill one and take it away to eat, not even if he's incredibly hungry – not even if he's incredibly hungover and wants the foxy equivalent of a full English with egg, bacon, baked beans and double black pudding. He's not going to stroll in, eye up a buxom chicken with nice big breasts, think, Hmm, I fancy that one, and leave it at that. He's going to go into a frenzy of killing that would make Quentin Tarantino go a bit green around the gills, but then walk off with just one chicken for dinner.

They don't just eat chickens; they eat babies, too, given half a chance. It's them or us. So you have to kill 'em.

We kept a shotgun on the smallholding for killing rats. It was perfectly legal, but I wasn't a very good shot. I was out shooting rats one day when I saw a fox lurking around not too far from me. Foxes, unfortunately, are a lot bigger than rats, and this wasn't a very powerful shotgun. I took a shot, hit it – just – but only wounded the thing. It skulked off, crawling up the hill and hiding behind some trees.

Now I might have hated the animal, but even I didn't want to leave him in pain to die a grisly death, so I decided I had to finish him off. I felt like the deerhunter – all I needed was 'Cavatina' playing in the background and you'd have been hard pressed to tell the difference between me and Robert De Niro. (Apart from the fact, I suppose that I was in leafy Kent hunting a fox and not in the Pennsylvania backwoods hunting a giant stag!) I started to track the fox by following the trail of blood. I wasn't particularly looking forward to finding it and looking it in the eye, but I did wonder what it was going to be like – I knew I'd have to shoot it in the head because it was such a small gun and that would be the only way to kill it quickly, unless

I clubbed it to death, which would have been pretty drastic!

Eventually I found it, and the thing was already dead. So ended my career as a fox hunter. But I would, happily and with a clear conscience, ride to hounds. Unfortunately I would be more likely to give the foxes a bloody good laugh than send them off to meet their maker, as I am about as unskilled a horseman as you are likely to find.

This was brought home to me on a recent holiday in Barbados. I was staying in a hotel and I arranged to take my two sons on a twilight horse ride along the beach. It was to be a lovely evening – we were to trot along the golden sands, past all the most expensive hotels in Barbados and then trot back as the sun sets magnificently over the horizon. I called the stables. 'Will you be needing large horses, sir?'

'Well, I'm sure just ordinary-sized horses will be fine for my sons,' I told the man. 'But for me, you'd better find the biggest, fattest horse in the whole of Barbados.' Sure enough, when we were introduced to our steeds, I was led towards Kaleidoscope, the Frank Bruno of horses – a huge brute of an animal.

'Don't worry,' said our guide when he saw me eyeing the beast with some apprehension. 'He's got a lovely nature.'

Kaleidoscope snorted at me.

'Have you done any riding before?'

I coughed a bit nervously. I'd told the kids, of course, that I was an expert horseman, the dead spit of Frankie Dettori, in equestrian ability if not in frame. 'I've done a bit,' I mumbled in what I hoped was a modest-sounding voice.

'Good,' he replied. 'The thing about Kaleidoscope is that he sometimes needs reining in a bit.'

'Reining in. Right,' I replied, wondering what the hell that meant.

Off we set. Everything was going swimmingly, although my nerves were not helped when our guide explained to me that there was a big horse-racing tradition in Barbados, and that Kaleidoscope had, on a number of occasions, won their equivalent of the Grand National and was now a sort of rescue horse. As we started the return journey, the tide started to come in and we were forced to ride closer to the edge of the beach, in spitting distance of the hotels, where there were little rough-hewn stone walls leading down to the sea.

All of a sudden, Kaleidoscope has a flashback of winning the Barbados Grand National and sees the low wall as something like Becher's Brook. He breaks out of line and hurls himself over the jump. As I looked, terrified, to the side, I was treated to the sight of Michael Winner and Wayne Rooney, both sitting on the terrace of a hotel restaurant, open-mouthed and somewhat agog at the sight of this slightly corpulent, lobster-red man fly past on this monster of a horse, holding on for dear life and yelling, at the top his voice, 'Chriiiiiiiiiisssssstttt!!!!!!!!'

I was so frightened I seized up. The horse jumped the wall perfectly, but I was holding on to the reins so tightly that I broke the tendons in one of my fingers – so badly that the end of my finger was pointing off at an angle to the rest of it. My wine-induced attempts to knock it back into line at the dinner table that night were ill advised and, back in London, I ended up with something that looked not unlike a sex aid strapped to my middle finger – embarrassing when you find yourself on national television interviewing a highbrow politician, only to look like you're giving him the finger in the most spectacular way imaginable.

So as you can imagine, if this is what happens when I'm taking a gentle trot along the beach, my presence in a hunt will not exactly strike fear into the heart of even the most plodding fox. But I would defend the right of fox hunters to continue their pursuit to the last. Foxes are a pest and a menace, and this ridiculous ban is a patronising assault on the country way of life by a townie government that simply does not understand the ways of the country. It is an assault on people's liberty, and I admire those members of the government – such as Kate Hooey – who took a stand and declared publicly that she thought it was wrong.

A final thought. Every aspiring Labour government for I don't know how long has said they would ban fox hunting. Blair did it in his manifesto, and then spent years trying to dance around it because he knew it would lose him votes in the shires. In the end he just ran out of wriggle room. But consider this: ten times more parliamentary debating time has been spent discussing the fox-hunting ban than was spent debating whether or not we should go to war with Iraq. Think about it. For every hour that was spent discussing our involvement in a war that to date has cost the lives of so many British and American servicemen and God knows how many countless thousands of Iraqis, ten hours was spent discussing foxes. No matter which side of the fence you fall on, that has to be wrong. Hasn't it?

Why should I love my bum? Nobody else does...

The advertising industry has to be up there with prostitution as the most morally repugnant business there is – although it is true that the money is slightly better if you go into the selling of soap powder, dog biscuits or cat chews as opposed to your body.

I was shopping in a supermarket the other day, and I couldn't believe one particular advertising slogan which read as follows: 'Love Your Bum'. This was for a particular brand of toilet tissue, and it got me wondering about the process whereby they brainstormed that particular slogan.

Picture the scene: a long boardroom and a

series of pony-tailed executives in dark suits and polo neck sweaters, all sitting round the glass-topped table drinking double decaf lattés and mineral water and sucking on Fox's Glacier Mints. Their brief? How to make a particular brand of toilet tissue more attractive to shoppers, and so sell more, and so make more profits for the shareholders, and so make everybody think this particular advertising agency is a bunch of geniuses. A series of lunches would then result in various slide presentations, flipcharts, coloured diagrams, coloured graphs and goodness knows what else. The creative juices of these supposedly fine minds are allowed to run free until we are eventually left with a slogan of unparalleled 'brilliance' – a heartfelt request to love your bottom.

I have to tell you – even though you may not want to know – that in my life various people have been strangely attracted to various parts of my anatomy, but I think I am on fairly safe ground when I state quite definitively that no one has been ever been particularly enamoured by my backside. The idea that I will suddenly swoop on a packet of toilet tissue simply because I have been told that to do so will allow me to love my bum just leaves me speechless.

But it doesn't end there. Recently, a major bank started an advertising campaign based on the strapline: 'We love to rock and roll'. How much more ludicrous could that possibly be? If I deposit my money with a bank, I want to know that it's secure. I want to know that skilful executives are trying to make as much interest from it as possible, that they are making scrupulously wise investments, that they are there twenty-four hours a day, seven days a week, guiding me what to do with it. I want them to be dull. I want them to be boring. I want them to be sensible. I am not in the least bit excited by the prospect of them standing on their desks with their ties around their heads dancing to the latest sounds while naked ladies walk around carrying silver platters of cocaine for their enjoyment. I don't *want* my bank to rock and roll. I don't *want* to go in to meet my area manager to be told, 'I'm afraid he's a bit busy at the moment checking out the new Chaka Demus cut, and then he's going partying with Lemmy from Motörhead, Jordan and a couple of chicks from S Club 7.'

It is plainly ridiculous. And banks are not the only guilty parties. What about the whole series of adverts on television that show that bloke reaching an almost climactic level of glee because he's managed to get the bathroom clean for his girlfriend by using a particular cleaning product. Does that correspond to anything anybody recognises in real life? Most men think they're being almost neurotically hygienic if they remember to lift the loo seat. Or, at the other end of the scale, what about the young women who, as soon as that time of the month comes around, decide it's time to start driving around cross country in an open-top Jeep, attend aerobics classes in an impossibly skin-tight leotard and participate vigorously in volleyball matches before dancing the night away with a series of different hunky men at a beachside bar? Am I the only one that thinks it's far more likely that they'd be slobbing out on the sofa in a pair of comfortable, but unflattering, tracksuit bottoms, eating a family-sized bar of Dairy Milk and watching endless reruns of *Sex and the City* with a hot-water bottle clasped to their stomach?

No, I have become firmly convinced that advertising exists for one reason and for one reason only: to keep people in employment who wouldn't have a snowball's chance in hell of getting a job in anything else. Years ago, when I was working for the Fox Television station in New York, myself and a number of other executives were gathered around a table trying to sort out a series of adverts that were going to run in the New York newspapers. The advert was getting more and more complex as we tried to get smarter and smarter with our different lines, suggestions, use of pictures and just about everything else. We all thought we were being so brilliantly clever with our piquant double entendres and were convinced that our clever devices showed how terribly witty and ironic we were. However, the advert itself was getting further and further away from the point until the most senior of the executives suddenly slammed the table with the palm of his fists, opened the *New York Post* and showed us all an advert for McDonald's. It read: 'Burger, fries and a drink – $1.99'.

'That,' he said, 'is true advertising. It's simple, and everyone gets the message.' And the more you study the sort of ads we see today, the more you realise this is true. Think of almost any advertisement you've recently seen on television, heard on the radio or seen in the papers and you will notice they are becoming increasingly complex. Indeed, at times they seem to have absolutely no relevance to the subject whatsoever. Remember the one for a tyre company with a giant fat Buddha of a man standing in the middle of the road with his head covered in spikes wearing bondage gear while thunder and lightening broke around him and the sky was full of massive ball bearings. Why the hell does that mean I have to go and buy a particular brand of tyre? In fact, I honestly can't remember which brand it was advertising.

It's always interesting when I have conversations on the radio about the power of advertising. I enjoy giving callers a certain catchphrase or slogan from a brand – eight times out of ten a listener will have trouble remembering what it's actually for. You can try and play now if you like. Who or what was a Humphrey? What were those famous squeaky-voiced tin Martians actually advertising? The impeccably cool actor Rutger Hauer advertised a particular drink, but what was the brand? The amazing grinning dog lying by the fireside won a stack of awards – what was he, she or possibly it selling? And Orson Welles was famous for appearing in a series of TV adverts in Britain, but again, what was he hawking? No problems if you fail to answer any of these questions. If you've struggled to remember just what all these products are, as I'm sure many of you have, you start to see why the sums of money some companies spend on their advertisements is close to lunacy.

I've been involved on both sides of the fence. I've both commissioned advertising campaigns and I have featured in them. Very recently, for the radio station LBC, they shot a series of advertisements with me in different guises and poses: one of them was me pretending to ride a canoe down the London underground and the other was me standing at the top of a police motorbike display team. Now here's a question for you: what do either of those two situations have to do with a radio programme in London? If you're as baffled as me – and clearly most of the viewers of the advertisement were – I'm afraid I can't help. But the experience did give me an interesting insight into the world of advertising and what the people were like. I get shivers down my spine even now when I recall an entire Thursday afternoon spent in a film studio in West London sitting in a small canoe that was actually balanced between two tables, reciting lines like, 'Well, it beats other ways to get around!' If they filmed me once, they must have filmed me fifty times, and before each take girls would arrive with make-up, hair, refreshments and just about everything else to try and keep me happy. When the director decided that the canoe needed a bit more animation, two men were employed to start rocking it gently, one at either end. Trying to deliver that line without roaring with laughter was very tricky indeed.

The other advert I made was the one that entailed me riding on the shoulders of two mounted police officers as if I was on the top of a pyramid as part of their motorcycle display team. As we rolled past the camera I had to deliver the line, 'Well, you all say you want more police on the streets!' Unfortunately, I was staring straight into the sun, the two lads on whom I had to perch had not been warned of my considerable girth and bulk, and the driver of the truck was slightly deaf so he always managed to drive past the camera either a little too quick or little too slow. Not surprisingly, this advert went straight to satellite TV and never actually made it on to anything terrestrial – not even a break in the *Tricia* programme.

What did all this teach about me the advertising process? Simply that it's all smoke and mirrors. Never casually believe words such as 'natural' or 'enhanced' – when you think about it, what do they actually mean? If you see a two for one offer in the supermarket, check out the price for the one – check it's not hugely inflated. There is no such thing as a free lunch – not even on an expense account in Charlotte Street, the heart of the British advertising industry.

Myrtle the Fresian: pin-up for the discerning heavy metal fan?

As a young man, at just about the time in my life when my secret reading matter really ought to have been the Harrods lingerie catalogue, I used to smuggle a very different publication into my room to read by torchlight after lights out.

There was certainly never a shortage of reading material in my house, simply because my father was a journalist. As a senior executive on the *Daily Mirror*, he had to keep up to speed with all sorts of subjects, so I could take my pick of any periodical – from the *British Medical Journal* to *Land Rover International* – that took my fancy. For me, as a pimply young teenager, there was only ever one choice: *Farmers Weekly*.

Now I hasten to add that my penchant for *Farmers Weekly* was not due to the fact that I wanted to cast long, lingering gazes at the centrefold of Myrtle the Fresian; nor were my adolescent loins stirred by the sight of frostbitten old farmers' wives with green wellies and stout walking canes. On the contrary, whereas my contemporaries found their male hormones were pumped into action by the sight of electric guitars and progressive rock bands with tight leather trousers and long hair, I was entranced by a very different sort of heavy metal. I longed for a tractor and a baling machine. What better way to display my manliness in front of a bevy of country lovelies, who would be putty in my hands once I'd finished shifting several hundredweight of well-rotted manure? How fabulous it would be, I thought, to have a bloody great bit of land up in Leicestershire and to spend my days driving bulldozers and diggers and God knows what else. I'd have a big barn and some Land Rovers. It would be just sensational.

And as I nodded off to sleep over a picture of the latest word in combine harvesters, I would dream of myself as a farmer. I'd have a huge farmhouse, with an enormous, merry blaze in the kitchen fireplace. My buxom, ruddy-faced bride would be sitting at the huge table with a large jug of fresh, pale cream and lots of happy children would be dancing about when I got home from tending the land with my faithful sheepdog, Tag.

Of course, it's not quite like that.

My passion for farming soon dissipated when I realised that the reality is very different. Farming is about turning out before dawn on a bloody freezing February morning to hulk huge bales of hay around a field on your own when you're knee-deep in snow; it's foxes and rats breaking into the henhouse and stealing your chickens and your eggs; it's impossible vets' bills – half the value of your mortgage just for them to come up and stick their arms up a cow's bottom (I know people now who would do that for nothing). I used to think that all I would need to become the perfect farmer was a thorough knowledge of my James Herriot books – surely it would just mean knocking about Yorkshire in an old Austin and having rather genteel little adventures. Little did I know that actually to be a successful farmer you need to have a PhD in organic chemistry so that you can work out exactly which phosphates or nitrates or other fertilisers you should be pouring over your tomatoes.

My point is this: farming is hard. You know that, I know that, the farmers know that. So why is it that farmers are always *telling* us how hard it is? I think it must be the first thing they learn when they go to farming college. The first two seminars they have to attend must be 'The Weather: How it Affects Farms and How to Moan About It' and 'Government Subsidies: Why They're Not Enough'. Drive through Oxfordshire or Warwickshire around election time and all you'll see is tractors parked up in fields saying 'Blair's Killing the Farmers', or declaring that the NFU says no to this and no to that.

I know that the odds are stacked against farmers. And I know that, no matter how much I admire companies such as Tesco, the reason that they are able to sell me my eggs at knockdown prices is because they are squeezing their suppliers – the farmers – as far as they can. In all likelihood they are being paid what they were twenty-five years ago. I have sympathy for their situation, but this is just the way that market forces work. And it's not all doom and gloom: thanks to the genius of the European Union, we now have this slightly peculiar set-aside scheme whereby farmers are paid to set aside a certain amount of land and not grow anything on it. That way, some Brussels sprout farmer just outside Antwerp will be able to continue growing his veg without any risk of competition. It's effectively being paid not to work – something rare outside of politics these days. It's nice lack of work if you can get it.

But farmers don't see it that way. Maybe it's because they too used to sit up all night with a torch and copy of *Farmers Weekly*, imagining how exciting it would be to be able to operate their own heavy machinery. Maybe *they* did have a penchant for Myrtle the Fresian. And then it didn't turn out like they thought. Perhaps beneath every whinging farmer, moaning about the weather and his lack of subsidies, there is a heartbreaking tale of broken dreams and lost opportunities. Perhaps we should feel desperately sorry for these people.

But here's the bottom line: we know it's hard, but if you don't like it, you don't have to do it. Give it all up. Sell your land – it's probably worth a fortune anyway. Retrain. Become a piano tuner.

At the very least you could flog your James Herriot books. And those back issues of *Farmers Weekly* might be worth a few quid…

"Actually, it's not a tacky logo, it's bird sh*t.
I just thought it looked cool."

Goat dung: the new black

What on earth has happened in the world of fashion? If it's not girls who are roughly the shape of salt cellars walking down aisles in Tokyo, Madrid or Milan wearing a combination of a traffic bollard, a coat hanger and a chocolate croissant – with the likelihood of it ever reaching the stores about the same as me becoming Chief Rabbi – then there's the image of grossly overweight men wandering around in the sort of kit that only an athlete in his prime (such as David Beckham, or indeed my good self) should be seen.

Let's return to the days of the fifties, where the woman of the house was in an attractive floral skirt cut just below the knee, waiting for the man of the house to return after a hard day's endeavour – she would greet him with a whisky and soda and a nice warm meal. She wore an apron and sensible shoes and delighted in talking about how well behaved the children had been, and how she was going to be making jam, and the next Women's Institute monthly meeting. Those were the days that made Britain great.

Children wore dark-coloured gabardine raincoats with their gloves on bits of string through the sleeves and woollen balaclavas; boys, even from the age of seven, had to wear neckties. Little girls wore pinafore dresses and would no sooner put a safety pin through their nose or navel than attempt to go deep-sea diving with a great white shark. Dad wore a sensible suit with a white shirt, a tie and a hat, and Britain was a safe place to be. When was the last time you tuned into *Crimewatch* and the attacker was described as wearing a Prince of Wales check suit, a white shirt, a Guards' tie, a sensible pair of black shoes and was carrying a rolled-up umbrella and a briefcase? This is my secret plan to combat street crime – if we all dress like this, we will all be good guys.

How on earth would our predecessors view fashion today – particularly men's fashion? How is it that the most obscenely unfit men seem to be the ones who clamour to go to sports shops and fill their baskets with utterly inappropriate clothing? In my new world order, only men who have competed in professional football up to and including Champions League level should be allowed to wear trousers that are cut off just below the knee. Obviously youngsters will be exempt from this ban, but my prime target will be those hideous, beer-bellied oafs living in Essex and driving Ford Mondeos who inexplicably seem to be under the misapprehension that they look attractive dressed in a West Ham shirt that is straining across their ample belly, sporting a tattoo stating 'I Love Mum' and wearing a diving watch that will be able to take them to a depth of sixty fathoms. How they think they will ever get any use out of that while watching West Ham and Ipswich battle out a 0–0 draw defies belief.

The other fashion crime for men are combat pants. Why is it that blokes seem to think they need to fit as many pockets and zips as they possibly can on their trousers or their jackets.

Does it actually ensure that they don't lose anything? I don't think so! They are just as capable or losing their car keys, wallet or mobile phone in this gear as they are in anything else. Again, if you are a slim-hipped youth of eighteen currently having trials with Tottenham Hotspur and have the toning and finesse of an Olympic diver, you can wear just about anything you like; unfortunately this sort of revealing, figure-hugging gear is generally favoured by blokes who are a cross between Luciano Pavarotti and Buddha.

The other male fashion crime is the baseball cap: quite why a man in his mid- to late fifties thinks it's fashionable to be wearing a cap with the Nike logo emblazoned across it or a slogan such as 'Go For It' is baffling. Decorum, taste and decency has deserted men's fashion. Can you honestly imagine Winston Churchill making his all-important 'We shall fight them on the beaches' speech while wearing a Ben Sherman short-sleeved shirt, a checked cap and blue Dr Marten boots? I think not.

Other fashion victims include the men who think they have to have a logo on absolutely every piece of their attire. If it has an emblem of a crocodile, a polo pony or a laurel wreath, this kind of bloke is happy to wear it. If I had the time and the ability, I would love to try to promote a logo of a piece of goat dung as the hot new accessory – it would give me huge enjoyment to see men standing outside pubs in city centres up and down the land and going on holiday absolutely determined to be wearing the latest polo shirt with the emblem of a pile of steaming goat turd in the full belief that it was the height of fashion.

This is one area where, tragically, the fairer sex seems to be no brighter. They're more than happy to cram anything from their feet to their bosoms into increasingly uncomfortable apparatus or designs just to get the look of that particular season. I would pay good money to see anyone actually copy any of the designs from the top names that come to London Fashion week or the Paris catwalk and wear that style to the their local Tesco or Asda. Imagine queuing at the Sainsbury's refund desk in the latest Vivienne Westwood or Alexander McQueen creation, complete with bondage chains, PVC and fetish gear, and then ask for a refund on a two-litre carton of milk that's gone off before its sell-by date! Or bending over the fish counter in a pair of high-heeled shoes that defy gravity and seem to be on the point of breaking your ankle and leaving you face down in a fat piece of haddock at any second if you lose concentration!

And then there's children's fashion. What do you suppose goes through the mind of a parent of a young daughter who buys her little girl a T-shirt with the slogan 'So many boys, so little time!' on it? This was an actual product from a leading clothing manufacturer that had been on sale for months and was only taken off after listeners to my radio show made me aware of their grave disquiet about this item, particularly as the story raised its ugly head at a time when a huge number of paedophile stories were circulating. A caller told me that she had complained to the store that the logo about too many boys was utterly inappropriate. I have to say that after we gave out the managing director's private phone line out and urged listeners to ring, they were very quick to remove that item. But the question remains: who on earth thought that kind of T-shirt was suitable for girls aged three to eleven? And why is it that parents today want their children to grow up so quickly? What's wrong with the great Ladybird range of clothing and sensible sandals. Children need to be children for a certain amount of time. They should not become fashion slaves or image-conscious label groupies when they have just about come off their mother's breast. Let them have their childhood with little shorts, little dresses and simple T-shirts, and just bring back basic designs.

My fashion world might be a reactionary one, and one that can be seen to be desperately simplistic, but when it comes to children's fashion I assure you it would be a made-to-measure success.

Why the Royal Family really should be a laughing matter . . .

A caller to my show accused me of being constantly against the Queen and permanently trying to find reasons to knock members of the Royal Family. This is quite unfair: it's really nothing personal. It's not the Royal Family that I have any problem with, rather it's the whole institution of monarchy.

To me, it is not only unfair, it's bordering on the downright scandalous that one person gets to spend his entire life living in a stinking council estate in Sunderland with little chance of ever having a decent job, lifestyle or even health expectations, while by an accident of birth another person ends up inheriting the whole of Cornwall.

You only have to see how the British Royal Family has managed to turn itself into something approaching a pantomime to realise that the idea of blue blood or true lineage is utter cobblers. Indeed, it's interesting that the Royals are so interested in horses: you have to wonder whether, if the family had been run along the lines of a stud farm, some of the current crop would have been moved away from siring duties and on to less important jobs – like pulling the milk cart. The immediate Royal Family is the biggest bunch of chinless, cosseted, indolent, work-shy individuals. And there is only one thing that annoys me more about the whole process than the family themselves, and that is the appalling, hand-wringing flunkies that attach themselves like leeches to the whole dreadful parade.

Good. I'm glad I got that off my chest.

Now to go back to the subject of this chapter, our sovereign, Queen Elizabeth II. For the record, I think she has done an amazing job and has been scandalously let down by her errant and dopey children. The Queen is clearly a woman who not only understands the maxim by which the British Royal Family has endured for years – namely that duty comes above all else – but she is also prepared to live by it. And to see her sitting at parades that can last hour after hour in the sweltering sunshine, watching half-naked Maori tribesmen perform a dance of welcome, or being forced to endure endless speeches from boring leaders at meaningless Commonwealth conferences, even I have a shred of sympathy for this diminutive woman.

I am equally as fond, if not more so, of her old man, Prince Philip. If I were running the country I would, given half a chance, put him in charge of all British diplomatic missions. Let's just look at his unique way of dealing with indigenous people. When he visited Scotland and came across a driving instructor, he asked him how on earth he managed to keep all the locals off the drink long enough to get them past the test. When he was with a group of British university students in Eastern Europe, he told them if they stayed there much longer they would all get fat bellies like the rest of the local people. He warned against staying in China too long because you can get slitty eyes, and once, when he was being shown around a factory and a particularly complex piece of wiring was put on display, he bellowed that it looked as though it had been put in by Indians! But Philip belongs to a different era and a time when an Englishman could call the world precisely as he saw it. It's totally unjust to suggest that he is in any way racist or sexist – it's simply the world that he knows and understands.

(Alongside him as leader of the British diplomatic mission, by the way, I would place John Prescott. The idea that our nation's interests overseas would be represented by the Duke and Two Jags – who would be ready to thump anybody in the chops if they disagreed with him in any fashion – is so marvellous I feel sure it would propel Britain back to the top of the industrial tree.)

Prince Philip has probably done more than any senior member of the Royal Family to maintain sovereignty in this country. Recall, if you will, the scenes that followed the death of the Princess of Wales. They brought out everything that is bad about the British Royal Family, who chose to seclude themselves away from their people to allow themselves to go through their own mourning process. While that is quite understandable – a part of human nature – I am afraid that if you choose to reign over us then you also have a duty to your subjects. There was enormous unrest over what appeared to be the hard-hearted aloofness and callousness displayed by the Royal Family when they stayed up at one of their countless estates (this one happened to be in Scotland) and the rest of the public gathered at two key locations in the capital: Buckingham Palace and Kensington Palace, where Diana had lived. The gulf between the Queen and her subjects had never been as wide. It almost appeared that they were sticking two fingers up at their own people and simply saying, 'Get on with it.' It was left to the not-inconsequential political skills of Tony Blair and his key advisor at that time, Alistair Campbell, to work out a deal by which the Queen could be coaxed back to London to give a TV address live with Buckingham Palace behind her.

But there was still work to be done. There was still the enormity of Diana's funeral day to get through and the possibility that some members of the public might actually start to turn on the Royal Family because they perceived it had both contributed enormously to the sense of misery and betrayal Diana had experienced, as well as appearing to greet her death with utter indifference. This is where the family's advisors and courtiers pulled off a blinding PR coup. Of all the images I can recall about the terrible days after Diana died, leading up to and including her funeral, few can be as stark and powerful as the one of Prince Philip – a man in his late seventies – walking alongside his two grandsons behind Diana's coffin, with Diana's brother Charles Althorp. These images told the whole story: the supposedly out-of-touch and ageing grandfather actually knew his duty both as grandad and as father-in-law of the nation's number-one cover girl who had met her death in such tragic circumstances. In that walk, the Duke of Edinburgh showed precisely why no one can match the British at pomp and pageantry. Amazingly, none of the four seemed at any point to have a tear in their eye: this was the genuine British stiff upper lip – the stuff of war movies and comic books, the myths coming to life in front of us all on the TV screen. The British Royal Family does not do tears: it does duty and solemnity.

The Royal Family will never recover from the impact that Princess Diana brought to this fusty relic. I remember spending countless hours and evenings as a reporter on the *Sunday Mirror* in a cramped red Mini Metro – not unlike that which Diana drove at one time – waiting outside her flat in Earl's Court with a series of photographers, hoping to snatch an interview or a photograph with the girl who had captured the heart of a prince. A very pretty but immensely shy girl, Diana, even during those early days, had a way of almost melting the heart of the hardest newsman or photographer, who might, in some cases, have been waiting the best part of fifteen hours for the chance to hear her say 'no comment' or giggle and turn her head at that extraordinary angle as she gently walked by, got in her car and drove off.

(Quite why newspaper editors think they need to keep reporters in these situations baffles me. Did they honestly think that Diana was suddenly going to walk out and, upon being approached by a reporter saying, 'Hello, I'm Nick Ferrari from the *Sunday Mirror*. How are you getting on with Prince Charles?', Diana is suddenly going to turn around and say, 'Well, Nick, I have been looking for someone to talk to about this. It's all going quite well and we have moved on from the snogging stage – but I don't think I ought to tell you any more about that. His granny is a lovely old girl, but spends most of her time watching the gee-gees and his Dad seems a bit fusty. Oh, and one of his brothers can't stop running around with the housemaid, and the other one spends a lot of time playing with his soldiers...'?)

The Royal Family's reserve and lack of emotion was subsequently to move the very fragile Diana close to a total breakdown, and the death throes of her marriage to Charles would be played out in countless headline day after day, week after week as the whole situation unravelled messily. I miss Diana. I put her on the front pages of newspapers and magazines and included her in more stories than I can count when I was a reporter for the *Sun*. She was great for this country – the envy of the world. There is no doubt that the nation, indeed the whole planet, is a lot sadder for her passing.

As for the other members of the Royal Family, I have considerable time for Princess Anne. Although she has clearly inherited her father's brusqueness and lack of patience and can be fairly candid when dealing with members of the press, I do think she is true to herself and seems exceptionally hard-working and, much like her mother, understands the duty of rule. The same cannot be said of her lofty, well-paid, well-fed brother Andrew. He briefly shone when he had the bravery to perform as a helicopter pilot during the Falklands War. It was subsequently reported that the Queen initially toyed with the idea of requesting that Andrew was not allowed near front-line duties, but she was overruled by her advisors and by Prince Philip. How he has gone from the position of showing the guts and integrity needed to fly helicopters during wartime to being a person whose only taste of combat is deciding whether it's a nine-iron or a wood on a celebrity golf course somewhere in Scotland is baffling, unsavoury and, unfortunately, a classic example of what can happen in the world of privilege where you enjoy a position not for what you know or what you can do but simply because of who you are.

As for Edward, what can you say? Someone who flunked out of the Marines, produced a ghastly, bottom-of-the-barrel moment for the Royal Family when he decided to stage *It's a Royal Knockout*, and then seemed to display that his greatest ambition was to make the tea for Andrew Lloyd Webber in his theatre group. The fact that he was given the earldom of

Wessex (an area that doesn't actually exist) when he married seems to sum up this trifling nonentity rather well.

If things go on the way they are, however, there's no chance that we'll ever be rid of this useless bunch – they are as much a part of the fabric of our life as wet bank holiday Mondays, Christmas shopping queues and the Liberal Democrats always being in third place. If you want to move on, you have to get radical. Here's my plan to get rid of the Royal Family without having to man the barricades or indulge in a bloody revolution. You simply point and laugh.

How does this work? It's simple. If you see a member of the Royal Family as you are going about your daily tasks, just stop, point and laugh very loudly. For instance, if you happen to be a nurse and Prince Edward arrives to open the new geriatric wing, as he is unveiling the plaque and saying a few words just walk past, point and laugh. If you work at a town hall and Mrs Parker Bowles arrives to plant a tree, as she is handed a spade that is so shiny you can see your own reflection in it and starts to cut the first sod, just stop, point and laugh. If you happen to be walking down Whitehall and you see the posse of eight police motorbike outriders, Range Rovers and support cars surrounding a limousine carrying the Duchess of Gloucester to the Savoy for some ghastly lunch, just stop, point and laugh.

Eventually, the Royal Family will meet one Christmas at Sandringham and they will say to each other, 'Well, how has your year been?' And as they all regale each other with accounts of how every time they go out in public people just point and laugh, they might eventually get the message and decide to do something else with their lives.

If my plan is not successful, consider this: we will have Queen Camilla. The subterfuge that was practised with the announcement that Prince Charles would marry Mrs Parker Bowles and she would not have the title of Queen was obscene. Even I, with all the constitutional expertise of someone who is half Swiss, could work out that whoever is married to a king in this country happens to be the Queen.

I think Queen Camilla will be too much for many British subjects to bear, and if you think back to the lack of excitement that surrounded their wedding, when the only people who seemed to get the slightest thrill out of it were Nicholas Witchel, Stephen Fry and Melvyn Bragg, you have got to ask whether the Royal Family will find itself in a very different place as and when King Charles and Queen Camilla ascend to their respective thrones.

"Listen mate… I've got some bad news regarding our local."

Technology? I'd rather go down the Dog and Duck

I'll come clean: I'm a Luddite. I'm afraid of computers. They lurk in the corner of the room, looking balefully at me, willing me to come and use them and then going spectacularly wrong in ways I can't even begin to understand when I eventually crack. They turn themselves off when I don't want them to, and then turn themselves back on again when I do. They tell me they have Fatal Errors and Illegal Operations. No wonder I'm scared stiff of the buggers. I admit it: the chips I'm most comfortable with come with battered cod and mushy peas and, as far as I'm concerned, a hard drive is a particularly gruelling trip down the

M1 and trying to turn on a PC is likely to get you arrested. And I don't think I'm the only one who thinks this way.

It wasn't always like this. Once upon a time I was at the very cutting edge, a young man with technology at his fingertips – hardly a budding Bill Gates, but not exactly the technological moron I am today. When the newspaper revolution happened in the mid-eighties, and Rupert Murdoch moved all his operations from the old site in Fleet Street to Wapping, we journalists were forced to embrace the new technology. I will never forget walking into this amazing, new, purpose-built newspaper plant. I'd never seen anything like it ever before – suddenly all the old traditions of Fleet Street had come bang up to date, and we were all told we had to throw away our typewriters and use the new computers that had been installed on our desks. A load of American computer whiz kids were brought in to teach us how to use them. They were incredibly patient – they must have been warned in advance that they were teaching journalists who were (a) bloody difficult, obstreperous and challenge everything you can think of, (b) trained to do the exact opposite of what they were told, and (c) likely to have solvent-, drink- or drug-abuse problems (so whatever you do don't let them near the felt-tip pens). Sure enough, they held our hands through everything we needed to learn: we were taught to log on, how to file our stories, how to send messages to other users – all very simple stuff. When they finished they asked us, in their American drawl, 'Are we all up to speed? Are we all good to go?'

Everyone nodded in uncharacteristic silence and politeness, apart from one old-timer, an Australian who had worked for Murdoch for years. 'Yeah, I think I've got it,' he said loudly. 'Just one thing – where do you put in the paper?'

Unlike our Australian friend, I just about managed to get the hang of the new-fangled wizardry. Unfortunately, things have moved on a tad since then, whereas my computer skills have remained firmly in 1985. I'm now awash in a sea of CPUs and dongles; the first time I heard someone say the word motherboard, I thought he was swearing at me. Now my kids drive my computer. I have to write a lot of articles, and they all have to be delivered by email or by Internet or whatever magic it is that gets my words into the papers, and they all have to be copied and pasted and tweaked and highlighted and goodness knows what else – I live in absolute fear of there being a glitch, because if there was one I'd be as much use as an inflatable dart board. Thank God the kids are there to sort me out, even if I do have to put up with the sort of pitying looks they might give an elderly, incontinent dog. 'Never mind, Dad, you put your feet up and have a nice cup of milky tea. We'll sort this out for you.' Some people even send me emails. They must be mad. They're surprised when they don't get a reply and think I'm being rude, but I'm not – it just means that my sons are out...

Sometimes, even my sons can't help me – making it perfectly clear in my mind that computers are beyond the control of any man. Years ago I used to have a nice little sideline in standing in for colourful Tories: I was Edwina Currie's deputy on Radio 5 Live, and I also stood in for David Mellor if he was on holiday during his stint writing a column for the *Sunday People*. One day the editor rang me up and asked me to stand in for David. 'I'd love to,' I told him, 'but I'm flying to Vegas with my family for a holiday.'

'Don't worry,' he said with an insouciant disregard for geographical hindrances that would have been unthinkable a few years previously. 'You'll have the papers. File it when you get there.'

So off I went, feeling every bit the roving reporter, and I wrote my column on the flight over. When we arrived in Vegas, my sons agreed to help me email the column back to London. We met in the conference centre and they tapped away at my laptop with the deftness of a concert pianist. 'There you go, Dad,' they told me. 'Just click send.'

I bravely tapped the mouse. As I did so, all the lights in the room dimmed; the nearby slot machines stopped whirring; and my computer switched itself off. There was a noise that sounded like a generator in a science fiction movie switching itself off. Seconds later, the lights came on again; the slot machines sprang once more into life; and my column was nowhere to be seen. Gone. Lost in the ether, leaving me with the familiar feeling of wanting to throw the bloody computer out of the window. It is a feeling that I have revisited many times since.

That wasn't the only time I've fallen foul of technology while nobly pursuing the truth in the name of a Sunday tabloid. In the early days of mini cassette recorders, I was despatched to follow up a story. Word had reached our ears that a senior female member of the Royal Family, who can't be named for fear of giving my lawyer the cold sweats, had been having a little indiscretion with a policeman. The policeman's wife, we had learned, was less than happy with the situation. I was wired up with a discreet microphone and a tape recorder and sent off to secure an interview with her.

The photographer and I arrived at her house and he hid in the bushes. (A word of advice from an old hack: if you ever find yourself in the situation of being doorstepped by a tabloid journalist and they step to one side as you open the front door, it's not to enable you to get a suntan. It's so that the photographer who is doubtless hiding out somewhere can get a good shot...) I knocked on the door and she answered, looking slightly bedraggled, and holding a small, yapping cocker spaniel. 'Hello,' I introduced myself. 'My name is Nick Ferrari from the *Sunday Mirror*...'

'I don't want to talk to you,' she said abruptly.

'Yap, yap, yap,' added the cocker spaniel.

'Look,' I explained as reasonably as I could, 'if you don't talk to me, I'm only going to keep knocking on your door and making myself a real nuisance. Just give me a couple of minutes of your time, and I'll be on my way.'

She shuffled reluctantly. 'Well, what is it you want to know?'

'Yap, yap, yap,' the cocker spaniel echoed her question.

And so I asked her all the questions I had up my sleeve. 'Is this a very difficult time for you?' 'Yes, it is.' (Yap, yap, yap.) 'Don't you feel terribly betrayed?' 'Yes, I do.' (Yap, yap, yap.) 'How do you feel when you look at members of the Royal Family?' 'I can't bring myself to do it.' (Yap, yap, yap.) And so on – in the end the interview lasted nearly ten minutes, which for a tabloid journalist is pure gold.

When I arrived back in the office, everyone was waiting for me with bated breath to see what I had come up with – the editor, the lawyers and the senior executives all knew that this could be the story of the year. With great trepidation I took my hi-tech tape recorder out of my pocket, placed it on the table and switched it on. Breathlessly, we listened to what I'd got.

It started off with a lot of heavy breathing. That was me – the microphone was obviously a bit too sensitive. Still, it wasn't the questions that were important, it was the answers, so we all listened carefully to what she had to say.

Unfortunately, we couldn't hear a word of it. The only thing the microphone had picked up was the bloody cocker spaniel, yapping away every time the old dear said something. Needless to say, my colleagues were less than impressed, though at least they had the good grace to blame it on the tape recorder and not on me. Perhaps, being men of a certain age, they were thinking, There but for the grace of God go I. And there was no denying that yours truly had been foiled again by his total ineptitude with technology.

But I can't honestly say I lament my ignorance. As far as I can tell, computers are responsible for taking all of the romance out of the modern world.

Newspapers are a case in point. When you see an old film about journalists, you want to see the thumping on the typewriters and the rumbling of the presses. When I was a kid and used to go and see my dad, who eventually rose to be Executive Editor of the *Daily Mirror*, if you arrived at the office at half three in the afternoon it would be mayhem – the copy-editors shouting across the huge rooms at the top of their voices, the journalists manically tapping away at their typewriters. And then, at a quarter past four, this great grinding boom would start from the depths of the building – that was the presses rolling into motion indicating that they had started printing the paper. It had excitement and passion – it was like a theatrical production and it seemed impossibly glamorous. Now you go into a newspaper office and it has been taken over by these tiny little machines making a slight whirr. It's like working in Norwich Union – only with a bit more swearing.

And it's destroying office relationships as well. People email someone at the next desk to say they've had a call, or to find out where they're going for lunch, or to see if they fancy a swift half after work. What's wrong with kicking back your chair, putting on your coat and announcing, 'I'm off down the Dog and Duck, if anyone wants to come?' (By the way, I've always thought that if I ran a pub, I'd call it the Queen's Legs. Why? Well, everyone's heard of the King's Arms, but the appeal of a group of blokes waiting outside at 10.55 in the morning being asked, 'What are you up to?' and replying, 'Waiting for the Queen's Legs to open...' is enormous.)

Occasionally, when I've blown up my computer at home, I have to go to one of these Internet cafés. They are the strangest places in the world. You sit down with a bunch of people with whom you could easily have a nice chat while you drink your cup of tea and eat your chocolate muffin, but of course nobody says anything whatsoever to each other. They sit there in their own little cocoon, avoiding even making eye contact with anybody else, and have intimate conversations with people at the other end of the world. I can never resist wondering who they're talking to. Someone masquerading as a twenty-five-year-old Polish girl who likes to give corrective lessons, but is in fact a forty-five-year-old, pot-bellied farmer from Denmark pleasuring himself as he types with one hand, most likely.

It's only going to get worse. Soon people won't talk to each other at all, and the human race will evolve to have no mouths (we won't need them, after all), hunched shoulders, square-shaped eyes, flat bottoms but extra-strong fingers – all the better to tap hundreds of emails every day.

Why I feel like Kate Moss in the flyovers...

Let's say you fancy a fight.

Don't get me wrong – I'm not suggesting you *should* have a fight. In fact, if you *do* fancy a fight, might I suggest that you count to ten and then go and have a nice cup of tea and a sit down? Treat yourself to a chocolate digestive. Relax. Calm down.

Better?

Phew.

So let's say you fancy a fight. Down the pub. Who would you rather have helping you out: a Frenchman, an Italian or an American?

Not a Frenchman, obviously. He'd go on strike the minute it all kicked off and then start whinging about his beer quotas. And clearly you couldn't trust an Italian: they've hardly set an exemplary precedent in such matters. You want someone who's going to be with you all the way, not turning tail and fleeing the moment things get ugly. They might make a mean pizza, the Italians, but fisticuffs is not their forte.

No, give me an American any day of the week. Dogged, loyal and gung-ho, it's Uncle Sam you want on your side in a fight, someone for whom victory is all and defeat is not an option.

I like Americans. OK, so they get things wrong. In fact, sometimes they get things *spectacularly* wrong. But the thing about our cousins across the pond is that they get things wrong for all the right reasons.

Let's take Iraq. Wrong, wrong, wrong. It's a chain they'll be wearing round their neck for years to come. But they got it wrong for the right reasons. There *was* an evil dictator, who *was* dropping people into plastic-shredding machines, who *did* have political opponents murdered, who *was* capable of invading another country unprovoked, and who *did* gas people at will. Unfortunately, the oil question got mixed up in the whole affair, and that, of course, is a wrong reason for going to war; but the right reasons were there.

They are infuriatingly insular in their nature. When my children were at school in America, I'm not sure the teachers could even spell geography, let alone teach it. They seem to have no real interest about what is going on outside the United States, unless they find themselves in Vietnam. Even middle-class, moderately affluent families spend their entire lives without leaving the US. If they want to ski, they go to Colorado; if they want sunshine, they go to Florida; if they want wide, open plains they go to Idaho; and if they want to get robbed they go to Detroit. It's not right – people should travel – but again they do it for the right reasons. They are fiercely patriotic. If you go to any town in America and abuse the flag, they will go absolutely, bona fide nuts. Some people say this is simple-minded; I think it's bloody great. They have a fantastic belief in and sense of pride about their own country, which is something we Brits should really learn from.

Even their president embodies these two sides

to the American nature. OK, he sometimes mangles his words. OK, he can't kick his shoes off, watch TV and munch a pretzel without crashing to the ground and nearly choking. OK, he has an unfortunate habit of opening his mouth and making himself seem like a total buffoon. I am particularly fond of a story Sir Trevor McDonald tells. When he asked President Bush a particularly searching question, Dubya answered by saying, 'I know what you are. You're one of those TV reporters who ask tough questions.' Given that Sir Trevor had two cameramen, a sound crew, lights and a producer standing around him, this suggests that the most powerful man in the world has a penchant for stating the bleedin' obvious.

But joking aside, it sickens me when I hear people saying how incompetent and how damn stupid President Bush is. He's not. He's a two-time president – that's as good as you can get in American politics – and he's clearly got something to him that enables him to be re-elected like that. I like him and support him because he is there for the American people. He won't sign the ridiculous Kyoto treaty because he knows it would cost jobs, put petrol prices through the roof and make a lot of Americans very unhappy. He is a domestic president. He might get unstuck when it comes to international politics, but once more it's for the right reasons: he's got his eyes set on making things right at home.

An amazing PR job has been done in America. It's a vast land mass with places that are more different to each other than you can possibly imagine. Take New York and New Orleans. Two more different types of America you could not believe. New York is sophisticated and fast-moving, and New Yorkers like to think they're the smartest town in the world; now rebuilding itself, New Orleans was slow, relaxed and far from sophisticated. And yet people from both cities would respond to exactly the same patriotic devices – the Stars and Stripes, Uncle Sam, Apple Pie, America the Free – that give these disparate peoples a real sense of nationhood. The Cajuns of Louisiana have nothing in common with the smart Californians, yet they all rally to the flag.

I lived and worked in America for some time when I was in the TV business. I went to a meeting once with a load of TV executives, and I was very low down the chain, representing local news for Fox TV. Everyone was talking about programming ideas when this one guy says, out of the blue, 'Yeah, but how will it work for the flyovers?'

Everyone else started nodding their heads. 'Mmm, the flyovers,' they agreed in unison. 'Don't know how it will sit with the flyovers.'

Needless to say I was totally confused – to me a flyover is a thing that stops you having to drive round Hammersmith Broadway – so at the end of the meeting I took a colleague to one side and confessed. 'I'm totally confused, mate,' I told him. 'What the hell are the flyovers?'

He explained that America is totally driven by the two coasts: New York on one side, LA on the other. The rest of America is the bit that the big hitters from the coasts just fly over, hence the flyovers. But the flyovers are important to the executives, because that's where the people live who watch the programmes, use the petrol and buy the burgers. The flyovers are looked down upon a little by such people, but personally I love them for two reasons – both associated with my girth.

The first is breakfast.

American breakfasts are the best in the world. But there is a science to ordering one. In fact, there's a science to ordering any meal in America. The first thing you need to know is that you should never order what's on the menu. It's very rude – it shows you haven't given it enough thought. I made the mistake when I was first having business lunches in the US of *actually ordering* the grilled tuna half way down the main courses. I was a laughing stock. What I should have done is say, 'You know the olives you do with the fettuccine? Well I want that on the turbot. And I want my vegetables steamed for seven-and-a-half minutes, not boiled. And I'll have a green salad on the side with a separate Italian dressing. And make sure the chef stirs the dressing clockwise.'

There is a similar etiquette for breakfast. It is absolutely de rigeur to order as many different foodstuffs in as many different colours as you possibly can. Think of it like Joseph and his Amazing Technicolour Dreamcoat: if you have a big plate of pancakes, you absolutely must have some coloured berries and a side order of pale cream. Then you need the yellow of the corn muffin. I hope you're not full yet, because there's the dark pink of the bacon and the white and gold of an overeasy egg. Oh, and plenty of black coffee.

American breakfasts, then, once you get away from the low-fat tedium of the New York health mafia and into the fat-soaked heartland of the flyovers, is a serious affair. It's also seriously big. Which leads me to my second reason for loving America: its stores have the biggest jeans and shirts you have ever seen in your life.

Allow me to refer you once again to the front cover of this book. You will observe that I am not slight of frame. Finding myself on the wrong side of the XL size range – XXL if I'm unlucky (or if I've had a few too many of those pancakes and cream) – I find my shopping options somewhat limited. I don't have a choice of style or colour: if the shirt fits, I buy it. I'm particularly stymied by Italian designers (another reason not to have them beside you in that fight) because they cut their clothes particularly small – surprising, really, given that you can get genuine porkers of Italian men. But when I wander round the clothes department of a Wal-Mart in South Carolina and hold up a pair of jeans so enormous that it must have kept an entire family of Chinese workers in employment for a fortnight, my heart leaps. I feel like Kate Moss. I feel like Twiggy. I feel like a genuine Slim Jim. These trousers are designed for those fabulous Americans with huge guts, massive arses, an enormous packet of Wheatos under one arm and several gallons of Coke under the other; they are not designed for individuals with my relatively slight, svelte, athletic physique.

With a spring in my step and a sparkle in my eye I skip off to the nearest diner for breakfast. I order pancakes and cream and muffins, and my absolute favourite: a dish of ham and eggs that they dub Eggs over My Hammy.

And they say Americans don't have a sense of humour...

"Well, it's only a motoring offence, but I feel like
making an example."

Porridge all round, and pass the apple sauce

I hope, dear reader, that you never have to go to prison. And I hope, of course, that *I* never have to go to prison. At the very least, I hope I never have to go to the sort of prison that I would like to see introduced for violent crime in this country.

Allow me to describe to you a day in such an institution. You would be woken early by the one stark, flickering light in the middle of your small cell illuminating a bed, a table and a chair. You would slop out, then be given porridge for breakfast. Throughout the day you would be allowed out to exercise for the bare minimum amount of time allowed by the regulations. You would go to bed early. There would be nothing else to do.

There would most certainly be no televisions to allow you to catch up on your favourite soap, nor gyms for you to work out in that would cost a small fortune on the outside. There would be no daily newspaper or three square meals a day: while I would not go out of my way to make the food revolting, I certainly wouldn't make efforts for it to be delicious. There would be no library and no counselling; visiting would be severely restricted and socialising discouraged.

It would, in short, be a very unpleasant place to be. Far more unpleasant than it is now.

Prison today is nothing like the punishment or deterrent that it needs to be. Why else would there be so many repeat offenders? Why else would people who know what prison is really like risk going back there apparently so lightly. Prison needs to put the fear of God into people. They need to know that if they commit a crime, it will make their lives substantially, desperately worse. At the moment it is far too molly-coddling: in the interests of 'rehabilitation', violent criminals are given art lessons, the chance to learn engineering, cookery and book-keeping. They have a video library that is the envy of Blockbuster. It's like being back at college, only you don't have to worry about where your next rent cheque is coming from, because accommodation is laid on.

I am fully aware of the theories that suggest you should judge a society by the way it treats its wrongdoers. But we have accepted the liberal claptrap about the redemption of criminals for quite long enough. The result has been increasing images of a desperately disturbing nature: old folk battered in some cases to death at the hands of irresponsible thugs. Don't buy this nonsense that prison should be about the three Rs of rehabilitation, re-education and reform: the word prison starts with a P, and so does punishment. There's also a P at the start of protection, and we deserve some of that from this violent scum. That's why you're there. The only thing these people understand is discipline, and the fact that discipline has gone out of so many people's lives is why we have been led into so many problems.

Moreover, at the moment we operate a sentencing scheme that is absolute madness. The way things stand, if you are given a five-year jail term, it doesn't mean five years. Assuming you are well behaved, you are given time off your sentence – typically up to half – so a five-year term is not a five-year term at all, it's a two-and-a-half-year term. Not only is this another means by which prison is turned into a much softer option, it is also a terrible kick in the teeth for the victim of the crime you have committed.

I would arrange things very differently. If my word were law, there would be no more three strikes and you're in. With me, it's one strike and you're in, and your sentence means your sentence. So five years would mean five years, provided you were well behaved. But if you step out of line, I would add time on to your sentence. Cause a fight over the porridge? Well done, mate, you've got yourself another two years. Jail is about punishment, not giving rewards, and I rather think that under such a regime the discipline problem that is so widespread in all our prisons would disappear pretty swiftly.

No doubt, of course, people will complain that under such proposals we would exacerbate the already existing problem of overcrowded prisons. Well, there is a very simple way to solve the prison-population crisis. It's simple but effective, yet not perhaps beyond the wit of man to come up with: build more prisons. And who's going to build these prisons? Well, I'm happy to announce that this is the one time that I would willingly relax the prison monopoly on boredom and tedium. Let's get the existing prisoners to build the new institutions that we so desperately need. It would be a sobering business for them, I think, constructing these fearful places where they may well be locked up in the future.

Everybody agrees that there needs to be prison reform in this county. The level of crime on our streets indicates that what is currently in place simply isn't working. But the emphasis these days seems to be far more biased towards rehabilitation than punishment, and the balance is clearly all wrong. Prison should not be a picnic. It should be horrible in order that those who are considering committing a crime will think again...

There is a long and noble tradition in the British justice system that the judiciary is separate from the government and there are clearly very obvious benefits to this, not least that it means the government is subject to the rule of law and cannot act illegally. However, it is not the only way of doing things. When Rudi Giuliani became mayor of New York, he enjoyed almost cult-like appreciation for turning round a city that was on the brink of lawlessness. He did not simply do this by putting more cops on the streets. He did it because he was able to influence the judiciary: he was involved in the appointment of the district attorney and therefore had a huge influence over the court system. There is nothing corrupt in this: it's just a different way of doing things, and one from which we could learn a great deal. Our legal profession is unfortunately peopled by a left-wing, liberal elite who believe that, when it comes to punishment, the toughest you should get is only offering a selection of two main courses on a Sunday, and holding back apple sauce with your pork.

I used to be a local reporter in South-East London, sitting in magistrates' courts in places like Greenwich and Dartford, watching the flotsam and jetsam of society. This ugly parade of humanity knew it only had to put a tie on and be polite to the magistrate in order to get off with a preposterously light sentence. But if we had a legion of chief constables up and down the land who could talk tough and had the power to act tough, backed up by a Home Secretary who talked even tougher and was prepared to take the fight against crime to the criminals on the street, we might start to see a bit of a difference.

But as it is, antisocial teenage offenders giggle as they are given a spell of community service. If I had control of crime and punishment, it would not be a laughing matter.

Make poverty history? I'd rather make Bono history . . .

Simon Le Bon tried to kill me with a baseball bat once, but that's OK. It's what you want from a pop star.

In truth, my experience with pop stars when I used to write about pop music for the *Sun* was largely positive, and the bigger they were the less difficult they tended to be. It wasn't always the case: there was the time that Elton John's manager showed me just how effective his left hook was the day after I'd sneaked into Elton and Renate's wedding in Australia and it ended up on the front page of the newspaper; and Julian Lennon was less than pleased when I decided to liven up a slow news day by suggesting before one of his performances abroad that he had become a recluse as he was terrified of being assassinated like his father. OK, so it wasn't true in the strict sense of the word, but back then that was all part of the rough and tumble of the newspaper business!

Then there was Elvis Costello. He wanted to kill me too, though I don't know why. Clearly somebody had told him that I was up to something nefarious. We all used to do it. If I found myself standing next to, say, George Michael, I would have no compunction about sidling up to him and saying, 'George, just a word in your ear. Watch out for that bloke on the *Mirror* – he's planning to write a story about your mum and how she's a bit of a goer.' It would be totally made up, of course, but it poisoned the water for the next time my rival wanted to get an interview. Somebody must have done the same to Elvis Costello about me, because he used to call me up when I was at my desk and tell me the precise way in which he was going to kill me. We even turned it into a little soap opera in the column – 'Elvis's Death Threats, Week Four' – but for some reason that only seemed to enrage him more.

It all came to a head when I was at a Bruce Springsteen gig. I saw him coming at me, dressed in his trademark black, and my first instinct was to run and hide. My colleagues, however, weren't going to be denied this delicious piece of entertainment, so they forced me to stay where I was and stick it out. Elvis went ballistic. He was prodding me and poking me and telling me how he was going to kill me in the most horrible ways imaginable. All the while I was protesting my innocence, but he wasn't having it. So I'd like to make one final appeal: Elvis, mate, whatever it was, I didn't do it. Please, can we be friends now? I don't want to die.

Generally, though, pop stars have been perfectly gracious. When I interviewed Lionel Richie at his house in America and he found out I was about to become a father for the first time, my twenty-minute interview was suddenly extended to nearly an hour (much to the chagrin of the nervous publicity agent wringing her hands by the door), while Lionel laid his wisdom about what to expect from impending fatherhood on me. And Sir Paul McCartney did exactly the same thing when I was expecting my second child.

But pop stars will be pop stars. It was at the Montreux Pop and Rock Festival that Simon Le Bon tried to demonstrate his baseball skills upon my person. Having flown over on a very early flight, I had no idea what was in that day's newspaper. Little did I know that the paper had dredged up someone from Duran Duran's past and run the headline 'DURAN DURAN NEED COKE LIKE A HORSE NEEDS HAY'. In all innocence, I breezily walked up to the band and called out, 'Hi, lads, Nick Ferrari from the *Sun*. Any chance of an interview?' Needless to say, the boys were feeling uncommunicative. Simon ran at me with a baseball bat, and I fled, ruminating on exactly what I would like to do to my colleagues who had omitted to tell me what they were up to.

But at least Simon was behaving like we want and expect a pop star to behave. Pop stars, in general, are here to look good, trash hotels, sleep with lots of women and sell records. Oh, and beat up journalists. They are most categorically not here to be political activists.

I blame Sting. In the twilight days of The Police, Sting was journalistic gold. There were lots of reasons we liked him: he was good-looking; lots of people liked his records, so he was bound to sell papers; he had quite a sexy wife and could have Tantric sex with her for fifteen hours; and you never knew when the band were going to split up, though it was constantly rumoured they were about to. So when Sting called a press conference, you went. One day he did just that, so off we toddled to hear what he had to say.

There on the stage with Sting was an Amazonian Indian in full tribal dress and a bone inserted into his lower lip. Sting proceeded to lecture us about the plight of the Amazonian Indians; this poor fellow looked absolutely lost, confused and for all the world like he would rather be absolutely anywhere else – he must have wondered what the hell he'd walked into. Sting, though well-meaning, just looked a bit silly.

He should be singing songs, not pricking political consciences. If we allow this to happen, the next thing we'll know is that politicians will have started to release pop songs, and while the idea of the next Christmas number one being Tony Blair and John Prescott crooning 'My Way', or David Cameron performing JJ Cale's

'Cocaine', is an intriguing one, I really don't believe it's something the great British public is quite ready for as yet.

So there we have it: I am heartily sick of being told what I should or should not do and what I should or should not worry about by a bunch of clapped-out, half-baked pop stars. And while I'm sure Bob Geldof's motives are perfectly honourable, I'm tired of being treated like a fool. The idea that because we all dance around in Hyde Park on a Saturday in June – and they also dance around in Philadelphia and God knows where else – that suddenly we're all going to feel better about ourselves and the world is going to be fine and we're going to end global poverty, is ridiculous.

And let's not kid ourselves: half the time, this pompous campaigning is just an excuse for a rather jaded and forgotten act to get themselves another blaze of publicity. Harmless enough, you might think, but the net result is that some kid, whose brains are in his voice or in his fingers, who left school at sixteen and who has about as naïve a political view as it's possible to have, finds themselves explaining to Kofi Annan the intricacies of international politics. This is a man who speaks more than five languages. He is perhaps the most skilled diplomat in the world, and certainly one of the most skilled politicians. He has received a Nobel Peace Prize. How must the poor guy feel, being lectured to about global poverty by Midge Ure?

I refuse to wear the Make Poverty History wristband, so people tell me I obviously don't care about global poverty. Of *course* I care about global poverty. I think it's absolutely bloody shameful that kids are dying in Africa, and that there's an AIDS epidemic, and that there isn't enough money and there's no water. It's a tragedy. It's wrong.

But *Bono*'s not going to solve it. And while there are still hundreds of perfectly good hotel rooms with perfectly good TVs, why can't he just do what he's paid for, act like a *real* pop star and go trash a few of them.

"The dizziness will pass. Your body just needs time to absorb the bill I've just given you."

Witchdoctors: alive and well and living in Chancery Lane

S ome people are frightened of the dark. Others
get the willies when they watch a scary
movie or read Stephen King's latest blockbuster.

Me, I'm frightened of lawyers.

Actually, let me qualify that. I'm frightened of
lawyers' bills.

No, come to think of it, it *is* the lawyers
themselves I'm terrified of. They're a sinister
bunch, practising their dark arts behind closed
doors, using language that none of us can
understand and charging fees that few of us
can comprehend.

A lot of people combat fear with humour,
so here goes:

A man walks into a lawyer's office. 'How much will it cost me to ask you three simple questions?' he asks.

'A thousand pounds,' replies the lawyer.

'A thousand pounds?' splutters the man. 'That's an awful lot of money, isn't it?'

'Yes, I suppose it probably is,' answers the lawyer. 'Now, what was your third question?'

I'm quite convinced that lawyers are the modern-day version of witchdoctors. They are the holders of arcane knowledge, and we all think we can't do without them. Witchdoctors mumble obscure incantations in an attempt to bemuse and befuddle gullible onlookers. Lawyers do exactly the same: they use words we've never heard of (a curious mixture of Latin and Voodoo) and sentences longer than the Channel Tunnel to make us think that what they do is far more complicated than it is. My favourite lawyers' word is hereditament. It means house, but of course they can't say house, because the smoke and mirrors would be destroyed. Instead of saying 'buying a house', they say 'acquisition of hereditament'. And just like the African tribes who not only let the witchdoctor get away with it but actively encourage and consult him, so we actively encourage and consult our lawyers.

It's brilliance on their part, of course, because it throws us completely off the scent. If any of us should think that we are foolhardy enough to do our own conveyancing, or write our own wills, or dip our toes in any way into the bubbling cauldron of mysticism that is the lawyer's domain, we are soon put back in our place by a blinding salvo of incomprehensible legalese that would have compilers of the *Oxford English Dictionary* scratching their thesaurus.

I knew a lawyer once who had developed a wizard wheeze to bump those fees up astronomically. Every morning he would get into the office at seven o'clock, at which time he would put in calls to five or six of his clients. His clients, of course, would still be gently snoring under their duvets; at the very most they were still pouring milk on their Rice Krispies or flossing a particularly stubborn remnant of last night's dinner from between their molars. So he just left a message saying he called.

When his clients arrived at work, they would return his call. He'd shoot the breeze with them for fifteen minutes, bill them accordingly, and as a result he would have made several hundred pounds before it was time for his morning cup of Nescafé. Nice work if you can get it!

For less inventive lawyers, there is a fund of well-worn techniques to get those bills up and running. Next time you look at a lawyer's account, take the time to read through all the mumbo jumbo and you'll see what I mean:

> **To:** Shuffling a few pieces of paper into a neat pile
> Opening drawer
> Putting hand in draw and removing paperclip
> Attaching paperclip to aforementioned pile of papers (duly shuffled)
> Picking up telephone
> Requesting secretary (billed separately) place aforementioned pile of papers into envelope and post to client
>
> **£1,000 + VAT**

Their other classic scam is to divide their day into six-minute units of billable time. They will tell you that this is their way of making sure that their bills are kept accurate and fair. The reality, of course, is that if they call you up (probably to discuss your last bill) and you're not there – a process that takes perhaps thirty seconds – that's a six-minute unit of billable time. And if you happen to have a friend who's a lawyer (I'm told there are some lawyers who have friends) and you call them up to see if they want to meet for a few jars after work, that conversation is going to end up on some poor bugger's account as a six-minute unit, probably charged to a nebulous activity such as 'client care'.

They can get away with this, though, because they've got us over a barrel. I learned this to my cost when I was viciously, brutally, callously fired from a previous job and it became clear that my employers had no intention whatsoever of honouring their contract. So I called in the lawyers. They swooped in, metaphorically speaking, like an administrative SAS (only a bit greyer and a little more rotund), threatened my opponents with a Beretta rifle full of legal mumbo jumbo, and I walked away with a spring in my step and a few extra quid in my wallet. Of course, I paid handsomely for this impressive display of legalised bullying, but who's going to complain about a few overpriced paperclips when they've got me a bit of well-deserved justice?

In defence of Christmas

Why are we so frightened of our own culture?

Why do we seem hell-bent on demonstrating and displaying at every conceivable opportunity that we believe our way of life is inferior to everybody else's? Why can't we be proud of what we have achieved? Take it from me, multiculturalism does not work. Now, I appreciate a statement as potentially explosive as that requires careful justification, and so here it is.

At the very heart of British culture there is a spirit of tolerance and understanding. People have been able to escape here from all sorts of oppression, repression and fear, whether it be the Jews escaping the pogroms of the 1930s, or the Irish escaping the economic hardships of their homeland the century before that. Britain has always – and quite rightly – held out a welcoming hand. And along with that welcome has been an understanding, backed up with a considerable amount of legislation, to allow all these differing peoples to practise whatever their beliefs may be. That is absolutely how it should be. It is essential that people living in this country should have the freedom to celebrate whatever ceremonies or religious beliefs they hold dear. Hanukkah must be permitted to stand beside Diwali, which must be allowed to stand beside Kwanzaa, and nothing should happen that would deter anybody from celebrating any religious festival.

However, where I differ from the current political ruling class is in one simple respect: Christmas takes precedence. Britain is a Christian country. Certainly the relevance of Christianity has decreased, but nevertheless it is there. Tensions are created by the lily-livered weakness of petty council bureaucracy, and the dead hand of local government peopled by a bunch of bed-wetting, panty-wearing, white, middle-class duffers who try to perceive slight and offence where none is intended and who go out of their way ultimately to upset everyone's life.

A good example of this is the recent decision by the authorities of Luton, who decided to change their regular display of Christmas lights into something called the Festival of Light. When pressed as to why they had made this bizarre decision, the council's defence was that they did not want to cause offence to other religions who did not observe Christmas. But there was not a single Muslim, Hindu, Sikh or Jew in Luton who had protested. Indeed, followers of those religions are as keen on the spectacle and the allure of Christmas as is anybody else. But we have allowed this country to believe that its culture is either inferior to others or needs in some way to be watered down, defended or altered to make it acceptable. This is preposterous.

Whenever I have a discussion on the radio about ceremonies such as this, it is often the Muslim callers who are the first to phone in and say that they enjoy the spectacle as much as anybody. In fact, I remember a brilliant caller once phoning to say he was in the novelty business and without Christmas his takings would be down by nearly two thirds. Clearly he had no conflict with his religion with regard to the ceremony.

So how is it that a nation, known throughout the world for its tolerance and clarity of thought, and who in the past has been called upon to defend the freedom of the western world, has allowed itself to be cowed in this way?

The answer is simple. The great race industry – which grows like Topsy by the day and employs an ever-increasing legion of lawyers, advisors and counsellors – perpetuates the myth that people of a different creed or skin colour are easily offended. This is nonsense, and is condescending to the millions of people who have made Britain their home. But the race zealots have tightened their grip in such a way that bizarre pressure groups spring up all over the place to try and repeat the myth that anyone in this country who is neither Christian nor white is getting a rough deal.

In the last few months alone, a bewildering

series of race-awareness initiatives have hit the newspapers. They have included the fact that a study group found not enough black and Asian people were going to football matches, so research had to be done as to how we could make more of these ethnic groups go to the games. Did it not occur to these so-called whizz kids that perhaps black and Asian people *simply don't want to go*? What is their solution? Are we going to have buses pulling up outside these people's homes, enforcers dragging them out, wrapping them in a football scarf and ordering them down to Stamford Bridge?

Another similar initiative came when it was discovered that not enough black and Asian people were using the parks. Suddenly there had to be turnaround in policy in places such as Dartmoor and the New Forest to ensure that they were more appealing to people of a different skin colour. How utterly offensive! Can these so-called advisors not get it into their heads that the only thing that anyone wants in this world is assimilation, not segregation – similar treatment, not special treatment. Yet all this comes from the very industry that's supposed to be policing this sort of issue.

The last of these great initiatives came when the Arts Council made it plain that they would no longer offer funding to the same degree if local theatre groups failed to put on more ethnically suitable productions. Taken to the extreme, this would mean that a community theatre in Sevenoaks would have to book a black theatre troupe putting on a gritty, realistic drama about gun crime in Harlesden if they were still to get their financing. The fact that the potential audience has no interest in this production whatsoever matters not a jot.

This is not to say that legislation concerning unfair discrimination or illegal practices should not be on the statute book. Obviously it must, and the toughest penalties should be brought against anybody who decides to pick on anyone else as a result of their skin colour. But legislation preventing this has been around for many years.

The sooner everyone in this country realises that the quickest way to equality is blindingly simply – just treat everyone equally! – the sooner any problems concerning racial and cultural integration will go away.

Why I'll take Clacton-on-Sea over St Tropez any time

If I had a bit more time, and crucially a bit more money, I'd start investing in swimming pools in Kent and Sussex. It's where the smart money is, thanks to the fantastic arrival of the marvellous phenomenon of global warming. Lovely. As I write this we've just had the most fabulous summer and a brilliant autumn – people were sunning themselves on the beaches of Brighton and Bournemouth in October. Absolutely sensational. You should follow my lead – pile into shares for Piz Buin, because before you know it people will be wearing sun cream all year round.

The green lobby makes me utterly sick. They

moan on and on about people not using their cars, not taking cheap flights, not doing this, not doing that. Well, welcome to the real world. People *like* driving their cars. People *like* flying to Venice for thirty-nine quid. They're always going to do it, and there's nothing you can do to change that. I've got five cars. Two of them run on leaded petrol, so I have to buy little bottles of lead additive to add to the unleaded petrol. One of them is a Land Rover. It's been in the family for a quarter of a century and has been on display at Brands Hatch. Nobody is going to tell me that I can't drive it around London if I want to.

What these interfering meddlers don't understand about air travel is that if they'd only keep quiet, they would achieve their aims far more quickly. Encourage more people to take cheap flights to Malaga and we'll soon nudge the average temperature in England up a couple of degrees. And when that happens? We'll all be happy to spend our holidays in Blighty, and we won't have to take cheap flights any more!

In truth, I don't really buy this nonsense about global warming. It seems to me – and, I might add, to a significant portion of the scientific community – that the global temperature changes we have seen lately are little more than part of a cyclical climate pattern. In Roman times, we were a wine-producing nation because the temperature was so warm. A couple of million years before that we were in the middle of an ice age. Climate changes because the earth wobbles on its axis in relation to the sun; it doesn't change because I decide to nip down to the newsagents in my 4 x 4 to buy the Sunday papers.

But now, of course, eco-paranoia infects every part of our life. Consider, if you will, the humble carrot. We were recently treated to a TV report featuring Prince Charles holding up the vegetable and championing its loveliness. Except, of course, that it was very far from being lovely. It was so gnarled and knobbly it would have made Quasimodo look like David Beckham; it had rough, dirty skin with pockets of mud clinging to it; it looked slightly hairy. 'That,' announced our future king, 'is how carrots should be.'

No it's not! I don't want knobbly carrots. They look horrible, and they're impossible to peel. I want long, straight carrots – orange, preferably, rather than black – that don't have little animals living in them and don't turn into compost twelve hours after I've bought them. I want all my carrots to look the same, and that goes for my apples, cauliflowers and whatever else I want to buy. The idea that I should be forced to purchase a hairy carrot or a misshapen onion at a vastly inflated price because it is 'organic' (whatever that means) is one of the biggest cons of recent years. They call genetically modified produce 'Frankenstein food', but it's the organic stuff that looks like a prop from a gory horror movie.

So not only are we not allowed to have a nice cheap holiday, not only do we have to eat parsnips that look like the product of Stephen King's imagination, we're now told we have to recycle everything we use. What a load of utter cobblers. The idea that I'm going to rinse out my tins of tomatoes when I've finished making my spaghetti bolognese is so unlikely it's laughable – I'm going to throw them in the bin like every other reasonable person – but there are people out there who take this ruling to the most ridiculous extremes. We've all seen them at the bottle banks, out there in the pouring rain that has made their cardboard boxes carrying their empty bottles of Blue Nun turn to mush, assiduously separating out the brown bottles from the green bottles from the clear bottles and clanging them into their respective bins. The fact that some bloke then comes along in a bloody great lorry, emitting diesel fumes and clogging up the North Circular, then pours all the different coloured glass into the same bin (this does happen – I've seen it!), hardly seems to dampen their ardour. No doubt the fact that they've fulfilled their eco-duties in the pouring rain makes them feel terribly good about themselves, even though they'd have been far more sensible staying inside with a piece of organic toast, lashings of vegan-friendly soya butter and a steaming cup of thistle tea.

So no, I won't be joining the green lobby, and I urge you all to do the same. If you want to fly the family to Lanzerote for tuppence ha'penny, go ahead; if you want to drive a bloody great Volvo around Chelsea, good luck to you (just don't forget to pay your congestion charge); and if you want to buy shares in BP and Texaco, fill yer boots. If we are to believe the eco-warriors, companies like that are our country's future:

they've got their finger on the temperature dial and they're turning Clacton-on-Sea into St Tropez. We'll never need to moan about the British weather ever again.

And if you ever want to buy a swimming pool, you know where to come...

Europe: nul points!

Europeans don't get on – it's as simple as that.

It's a shame, really, but we all know it's true. The Portuguese hate the Spanish. The British hate the French. The French hate the Belgians. Everybody hates the Germans. And increasingly, all of us seem to hate the whole idea of one integral Europe.

It's hardly surprising. The idea of an integrated Europe was originally all to do with trade. With that remit, I could understand how and why it might work, and I even vaguely supported the idea when Ted Heath took us into the European Community in 1973. Subsequently, Harold Wilson offered us the chance of a referendum on Europe and, although I wasn't old enough to vote, I was hugely excited about the whole prospect of being European. Not for the first time in my life, I was completely conned.

As a trading bloc, Europe is fine; as a single entity with its own anthem, parliament, cabinet, flag, money, defence policy and everything else, it frightens the living daylights out of me. Each country has earned the right to govern and dictate its own destiny, and that should not be taken away. The grossest example of this political folly is the single currency, which was actually forced in against the will of many European nations. Thank God for the common sense of the great British people who, not for the first time, showed Europe the way forward and decided not to adopt the Euro. Any attempt at a single currency for a land mass the size of Europe is lunacy. Why should the interest rate the bank is paying you on your savings or how much money you have in your back pocket have anything to do with the success or failure of the Portuguese cork harvest? Why should a group of Baltic fisherman be able to terrify a European banking community to such a point that they start talking about interest rate raises because the whole of Europe is teetering on the brink of some sort of mini-recession. It is quite blatantly a load of utter cobblers.

But it's also a classic example of a ruling political elite being utterly convinced that it knows better than the electorate. Witness the scenes when the French voted against the EU constitution. It revealed the blinding audacity of some of our elected officials saying we must *listen* to what the French said, but it didn't mean the constitution was over. *Of course it did!* One of the countries that in the past had been the most supportive of the whole damn stupid deck of cards had, at last, come to its senses and said no.

Unlike many an Englishman, I have always admired the French.

Don't get me wrong – that doesn't mean I like 'em.

Now I know this is controversial stuff, but bear with me. I know that many of you reading this will have suffered at the hands of either their air-traffic controllers or their dockers. They always know when to pick the worst time to strike – the classic holiday periods in and around late July through to August, or around the Easter holidays when people have to fly over their airspace to get to Spain and Greece. And yes, it's interesting that they didn't seem quite as protective of their airspace between 1939 and 1945 when, yet again, we came to their rescue and saved them from falling under the crushing step of the Nazi jackboot. They couldn't get enough of us then, could they? But wind the tape on a few years and they can't wait to block up the ports, close down the airspace and basically make life as difficult as they possibly can for the sons and grandsons of those who liberated their homeland.

And yes, I know that many of you will have innocently ordered a meal in France, only to be presented with a horrifying confection of snails, amphibian extremities, offal of the quality that you'd think twice about giving to the cat, and garlic sauce. But hear me out.

You have to admire the fact that they're a strangely pedantic race, and when they decide they don't want something they are perfectly able to dig in their heels. And so it was with Europe: the French are to be thanked for the stance they took over the European constitution, and for the fact that it has blown the whole sorry thing up. Thanks to my good friends the French, the only future for Europe now is as a trading bloc, a common market – which is what it was initially set up to be. We must retain all our trading links with the Commonwealth, with the United States and, of course, with countries in Europe, but we don't need to be in some sort of federal club with its own flag and insignia to do this.

That said, there is one aspect of European integration that has nothing to do with trade, and I wholeheartedly support it, despite the fact that it is riddled with corruption and is a bloated, self-serving farce. No, I'm not talking about the European parliament, but the Eurovision Song Contest. As the years pass, the parental host, Terry Wogan – as close to a broadcasting genius as you will ever get – becomes increasingly annoyed by the backhanded voting system, but the joy of listening to him splatter into his red wine with anger, demanding that something must be done, makes it all worthwhile. Terry, you are a genius, but I'm afraid you're just going to have to get over it because it's never going to change. And nor do we want it to.

A bit like Europe, really – we don't want that to change either. I just want it to be a place where I can go on my holidays, where the children get excited because you change your sterling into different currencies with the heads of different presidents or kings or queens on it. And I want it to provide a dazzling array of olive-skinned, finely honed young women – and the occasional bloke as well, I suppose – who are able to man all our restaurants and coffee bars with their swarthy panache. And I want to pay them in pounds.

"Excellent idea, Verger – introduce a little fear back
into the church."

Vote Nick Ferrari for Archbishop if you want the F word in church

Make me Archbishop of Canterbury, or Chief Rabbi, or Archbishop of Westminster – or head of any church you care to name – and I guarantee to get bums on seats. I'll have them filling up the pews once a day and twice on Sundays. The churches will be so bulging you'll think it's Christmas every day. I'll pack 'em in the aisles.

And how is this miracle to be achieved? Why do I think I will be able to do what the finest religious and philosophical minds of the past several decades have been unable to manage? Simple. I propose that we reintroduce a four-letter F word into the church, and that word is ... fear. We have to put the fear back into religion if it's to have any impact on our society whatsoever.

As with so many of society's ills, the wane of the importance of the church can be traced directly back to the liberalisation of the sixties and seventies. This liberalisation affected our educational, political and administrative systems in different ways, but the moment members of the clergy decided that they no longer wished to be raised on a pedestal above lay people, the moment they decided they wanted to be 'one of us', it was the death knell for the Church as we knew it. How can they be one of us? The whole point is that we turn to these people at moments of enormous stress – such as the death of a partner. Suddenly, these figures of authority, these people to whom we turned for advice, guidance and comfort, were wandering around the streets with big smiles strumming guitars. Our vicars became happy clappy and we started singing pop songs in church.

It shouldn't be like this. There should be something magical, mystical and ethereal about the church, something you can hold in awe. African tribesmen say that you should never look inside the witchdoctor's tent: you expect something wondrous, but the moment you see that it's just full of old goatskins like everybody else's, the magic is gone. It's the same with the church.

When I was a kid, we used to go on long European tours to visit relatives in Switzerland. We would drive through dirt-poor French and Italian villages where the roads were little more than dust tracks and the peasants' houses were falling in. The only place of any opulence, the only place that had any money whatsoever, was the Catholic church. In the midst of the poverty it would be gleaming with golden crosses, revered for its stunning architecture and imposing nature. The villagers, dressed in black, would be caring for that church like it was their own home, making sure the gold was shining and the Bible well looked after. When the holy father said something, people listened. Now, it can easily be argued that this was wrong – that the wealth of the Church should have been used to see that the villagers' lives were improved materially rather than spiritually – but there is no way you can deny that when the Church was imposing, when it had magnitude and magnificence, it had a far greater impact on people's lives. Now, because senior members of the clergy have this lunatic progressive attitude, the Church has about as much impact on the lives of ordinary people as a trip to Woolworths.

But does it matter? Well yes, actually, I think it probably does.

Our society suffers from a lack of respect, and it's hardly a great surprise. Who do we have to look up to these days? Not the Royal Family, certainly. With the exception of the Queen, who does a really amazing job, they have been proven to be little more than a bunch of adulterous playboys (and girls) with a penchant for shady business deals. What about our politicians? No, they're just the same – we wait for them to be exposed as liars and sleaze merchants. Sports stars? Well, you just have to pick up any Sunday newspaper to find out who they've been caught in bed with this time.

But surely we can look up to the Church. Can't we?

Unfortunately not. The one institution that, historically speaking, has always been there to guide us, to keep us on the straight and narrow, has become absolutely hopeless. Consumerism is the new religion – we don't go to church any more, we go shopping – and the institution that used to instil a little respect in us has gone to the wall.

I have done a lot of work on a BBC programme called *Heaven and Earth*. We had an item once about somebody who had managed to distil the Lord's Prayer into a text message that you could download on to your mobile phone. This was being roundly applauded by members of the religious community, and my view, frankly, was that they should have been excommunicated! Well, perhaps that's a little harsh, but I do believe that this was seriously demeaning a prayer that has meant a great deal to a great number of people throughout history. As young men were being mown down at the Somme, the Lord's Prayer was being said. As people watched the planes crash into buildings during 9/11, the Lord's Prayer was being said. As terrified commuters lay under rubble during the London bombings, the Lord's Prayer was being said. It is a source of strength for so many people, and now the Church, in approving its use as a text message, have done little less than ridicule it.

So come on guys, let's introduce a little more fear into church. When we were kids we loved Halloween. We loved the scary frisson, but we knew that Mum and Dad were close by. It can be the same at church: a bit of hellfire and damnation from the pulpit and a kindly word from the vicar afterwards. We all like being scared. We love watching *The Shining*. Why not take a few leaves out of Hollywood's books?

If you do that, I promise not to run for Archbishop.

Prince Philip in suspenders? Now that's entertainment!

The next time you're in a pub and man comes up to you dressed as a baby, or a chimpanzee, or a drag queen, or Harry Potter, and rattling a bucket, here's what you need to do: punch him.

Once you've punched him, and he's recovered from the shock, you need to say to him, 'Admit it, mate. You're not dressed as Harry Potter because you want to do good work for charity. You're dressed as Harry Potter because you have a deep-seated emotional problem or a psychological flaw.' It might sound harsh, but you've got to be cruel to be kind. He'll end up thanking you for forcing him to address his problems and seek help.

I can't be doing with these people who act in the most ridiculous fashion and claim that it's all in the name of charity. I'm quite convinced that if Saddam Hussein had donned a silly false nose and addressed the United Nations in a funny, squeaky voice saying that he was invading Kuwait as part of Red Nose Day, he'd have been given the Nobel Peace Prize. If Jeffrey Archer had said that he was meeting women of the night do discuss what japes they might get up to for Save the Children, he'd be Prime Minister by now. You can do almost anything you bloody well like nowadays, so long as you say it's for charity.

So now we find ourselves in the idiotic situation where the BBC will turn over its entire Friday night broadcasting to these daft events, and reporters are sent all over the country to cover the fact that the manager and staff of a bank in Kenilworth have all dressed up as characters from *Winnie the Pooh*. Well I'm sure all their hearts are in the right places but, as I may have mentioned before, I require a little more sobriety from my financial institutions. I'm afraid I would move my money straight out of any bank that was willing to have its manager appear on television dressed as a heffalump.

I used to work at Canary Wharf, where a lot of banks had their offices. I was quietly minding my own business in a bar after work one evening when a group of city bankers flooded in. They were on a sponsored pub crawl with a difference: there was a vicars-and-tarts theme to the event. To add an extra twist, all the women had to dress as vicars and all the men had to dress as tarts. Now why on earth would you do that? These were all people who had more money than they knew what to do with. Why not just write out a cheque for 500 quid and go and spend the evening with the missus – never mind raiding her knickers and stockings and having to go to some transvestite shop to buy a pair of high heels big enough for your hilarious costume. They don't do that, of course, because they've got problems! And, of course, they all think it's jolly good fun to be half cut and dressed as a hooker, but what about when they go home and their two kids see Daddy dressed like Marge Simpson with a pair of lacy fishnets and a Wonderbra? Think of the psychological damage! Think of the thousands you'll spend in counselling and therapy costs to make up for that little evening painting the town – not to mention your fingernails – red! Charity, remember, begins at home!

I get approached by a large number of charities, asking me to represent them in various ways, and I always tell them the same thing: I wish you the very best of luck, but I'm really not the right man for the job. I can't even remember my godchildren's birthdays; in fact, I'm not even entirely sure I can remember my *own* birthday; the idea that I'd provide anything of any use for a charity is beyond credulity. So I'll happily mention a charity event on the radio, or send them some signed merchandise, but the idea of being a patron sends shivers down my spine.

On a more serious note, we really do need to be careful about which charities we give our hard-earned cash to. Most of them – by no means all, but most – are a complete rip-off. One charity I could name but won't pays its managing director £100,000 a year and three or four other people £80,000 a year, and they have just spent £800,000 tarting up their offices.

Now nobody's saying these people have to work in a hovel, but at a time when they are also closing down hostels for the very people the charity is supposed to be protecting, it does seem out of proportion, to say the least.

The Diana Memorial Fund is another case in point. When she died, the nation was moved to give millions in the belief that it would be distributed to the causes that she held dear. But the fund then found itself in the midst of a dispute with a doll-making company and the result was a multi-million-pound out-of-court settlement that benefited the lawyers. So you have to be extremely careful where you donate your pound.

That said, there are reputable charities that I am more than happy to support. The minute the poppies appear, I am the first person to buy one. It's a cause for which I have the utmost respect. But running over Westminster Bridge wearing a Godzilla outfit in the name of charity is just self-indulgent garbage.

So there'll be no dressing up as a tart for me – apart from socially, of course. But I don't want to sound like a curmudgeon, so I'll introduce a proviso to that: if Prince Philip will borrow the wife's suspenders and join me on a money-raising pub crawl around the city, I might be persuaded to put my objections to one side for the sheer novelty value. I'd see it as my public duty.

Until then, I'm keeping my trousers on in public.

The laughing policemen

Nothing peeves me more than these moaning minnies who can do nothing but criticise our police force.

Because of my almost unstinting support of the police, mine was the first radio show to play host to the then commissioner of the Met, Sir John (now Lord) Stevens. We struck up a good relationship, and I was asked to speak at one of his retirement bashes. It's quite a daunting task standing up in front of 500 hairy-arsed coppers, but I'm pleased to report that the following story had them laughing like a drain.

When Sir John arrived at the station (mine, not his) for the interview, I asked him before we went on air if there was anything he would particularly like to say, any message he wanted to get across. 'Actually, yes,' he replied. 'Obviously I'll take calls about anything, but what I would really like to make clear is that we are not going to be closing down any more police stations. We've closed too many down, we realise that, and we know we've annoyed everybody, so we're not going to do it any more.'

'No problems,' I told him. 'We'll do exactly that.'

As the interview started, it was immediately clear that Sir John understood everything about performing on the radio. He was not in the slightest bit nervous, had a good strong voice, and quickly cottoned on to the one golden rule: keep an eye on the red light. If it's on, it means we're on air, so you would be well advised to avoid using fruity language, or saying exactly what you think of the wife. But when it's off, you can say what you want.

I kick off by saying, 'With me in the studio I have the commissioner of the Metropolitan Police, Sir John Stevens. I understand you have a message for London, Sir John.'

'Yes, I have, Nick,' he replied. 'Thank you for the opportunity. I would like to announce that there will be no more police station closures on my watch. We've realised that this policy is not popular with the public and we know that we can only police by common consent. Indeed, I want to be opening police offices in schools and supermarkets and community centres around the country.'

And so we go to our calls, the first of which is from Dave in Orpington. 'Morning, Sir John,' he says.

'Morning, Dave. How can I help you?'

'Well, my garage got broken into three weeks ago, and I phoned the police and nobody's been round.'

'I'm terribly sorry to hear that. Someone really should have come round to talk to you about it.'

'Yeah, well the trouble is, John, that I can't make an insurance report because I haven't got a crime number. I need to report this to a police officer.'

'Right,' replies Sir John. 'I'll see what I can do.'

'Well, can I report it now? To you?'

'Um, OK,' says Sir John, professional to the last. He removes an immaculate gold pen from his jacket pocket, takes a sheet of paper and goes about his business, for all the world like he was the duty sergeant in his local nick. 'Obviously I'll take your personal details off air, but can you tell me when the crime took place?'

'Three Saturdays ago, they broke into my shed.'

'What did they take?'

'My Flymo, my hedge-trimmer and, as they were leaving, they nicked the wife's gnomes out of the garden.'

'Value?'

'Well, I suppose the hedge-trimmer was probably about forty-nine quid and the lawnmower about a hundred and ninety.'

'Right.'

'Don't forget the wife's gnomes.'

'No, no, I'm coming to those. Did you see them at all? Any description.'

'Yeah, one had a little blue suit and a pointy hat, the other was holding a fishing rod and sitting on a toadstool.'

'Now look, Sir John,' I interrupted. 'I know the Met's got problems with detection, but surely your officers can find those!'

The next call was from Joyce in Penge. 'Sir John,' she says. 'I was very interested by your comment that you won't be closing any more police stations from today.'

'That's right,' he replies. 'Not on my watch. I can absolutely assure you that this will not happen.'

'I see. So how do you square that with the fact that next Tuesday, after 175 years of continuous service, you're closing Brockley police station, despite complaints from all the locals and a pressure group.'

Sir John was momentarily lost for words.

'We want to keep our nick,' continues Joyce, 'and you're closing it down on Tuesday.'

Fortunately for the commissioner it comes round to a break. 'Right, Joyce,' I say, 'you've certainly put the commissioner on the spot. We're going to get a reaction for you, but while we give him a couple of minutes to sort this out, let's catch up on the local traffic.'

The red light goes off and Sir John immediately turns to look at me. 'Well,' he says a bit ruefully. 'That's certainly pissed on the f*****g chips, hasn't it.'

How his detectives roared at that story, and I should point out it was a decision he inherited and had nothing to do with! The commissioner proved himself to be a decent, down-to-earth professional, let's hope the same is true of his successor, although his first twelve months do not augur well.

Obviously, though, the police get things wrong. And because of the nature of their work, when the police get things wrong they can get it terribly and tragically wrong. The majority of the time this is an incredible body of mostly young men and women who, for not particularly substantial financial reward, literally risk their lives on a daily basis on our account. And what makes me more infuriated than anything is those people who complain that we live in a 'police state'. I'd love to know just how they would react if they got taken hostage at their place of work, or if their kids were involved in a pub fight – I imagine that they wouldn't be able to call for the police quickly enough under those circumstances. And if they really want to know what it's like living in a police state, I suggest they up sticks and move to North Korea.

The current controversy regarding the police force is over the shoot-to-kill policy. While I do think that it was introduced incorrectly and too swiftly – if you are going to take on the same policing tactics that they have in Israel where they deal with Palestinian suicide bombers, you have to ask yourself if the situation here is as grave as it is there, and the answer to that is most definitely not – I believe it would be madness to remove it completely. There is no question that the police should be armed routinely, but you can call up an armed response unit in London in a matter of minutes these days, and there will always be situations when the police will have to have the freedom to shoot to kill. There's no point telling an armed police officer that he is only allowed to wound: a criminal with an armed response unit on his tail is not going to stand still and say, 'Here, have a pot shot at my leg.' They're going to run, and dive, and duck, and roll, and spin.

Clearly it can go wrong, as it did in the case of the Brazilian man who was shot dead at Stockwell tube station. But the bottom line is this: there are evil people out there who will slit your throat as soon as look at you, who will happily pack themselves with explosives and blow us all up. The only way you can contend with that is to have people who are willing to put their lives on the line. To do this, they have to arm themselves and they have to be prepared – and allowed – to use those arms.

"I don't tolerate bullying, Hernshaw, and if you persist in doing so, I'll have to transfer poor Spiggott here to another school."

Requiem to a flying blackboard rubber

Readers of a certain age will be well acquainted with the exquisite pain of a blackboard rubber, flung with the fury that only an irate maths teacher can muster, as it hits you squarely between the eyes. It is, to put it mildly, unpleasant. One of the greatest boons of technology must surely be that blackboards – and therefore blackboard rubbers – are becoming increasingly scarce, so this curiously British form of corporal punishment is, thankfully, on the wane.

Of course, playing bodyline with the maths teacher was not my only experience of violence in the name of education. We had a music teacher whose enthusiasms in this field were definitely on the wrong side of worrying. He would turn up to each lesson armed with what can only be described as a piece of dowelling. Its supposed use was for him to be able to keep time on the piano as we all sang along to the best – or worst – of our abilities; in fact, it was more often used to hit the back of our legs or, if we were particularly unlucky, the back of our head. To this day, I can't sing 'Jerusalem' without my thighs twitching with anxiety.

There is no doubt, I would hope, that most right-thinking people would agree that this sort of treatment of young children – or indeed anyone – is quite wrong and, thank God, it seems to have been largely eliminated from our schools. Unfortunately, we've now gone in completely the other direction. Far from being in the position of being able to inject a bit of healthy respect in their pupils, today's teachers frankly wouldn't say boo to a goose. Come to think of it, they wouldn't say boo to an oven-ready poussin, and with good reason: they're too scared of the potential comeback. Who in their right mind wants to risk their already meagre pension just because some kid can't stay quiet during geography? The result has been predictable: an awful, awful morass of kids, often from what are traditionally known as 'broken homes', or coming from homes where Mum and Dad are working flat-out just to pay the council tax and all the bills, come into a place where discipline has fallen by the wayside and where, if a teacher tries to instil a bit of it, he or she risks ending up in the magistrates' court on the suggestion that they've tried to abuse the child in question. More often than not the parents couldn't give a monkey's what's going on anyway, and the whole situation turns into anarchy.

And we're surprised that bullying appears to be on the increase. Well, we shouldn't be. But equally, we shouldn't just blame the kids. I'm quite convinced that the reason bullying seems a greater problem now than it used to be is that the society in which we live is less caring in general. And I don't accept any of this claptrap about this being a result of Thatcherism; it's just a product of how the world stacks up now. Look at Iraq. Our young people are given the inspiration of politicians – people we ought to be able to look up to – bullying their way into another country. Indeed, the bullying nature of the state is evident even at more grass-roots levels. I took a call from a lovely lady from South-East London. She had a couple of kids of her own, and worked as a childminder, taking other little ones into her house. Everyone was happy. Suddenly, a bullying state inspector turns up at the door to check everything was as it should be. He takes issue with the dolls – dolls that the kiddies had been happily playing with for months – on the basis that they were all white. He told the childminder that she had to get herself some black or Chinese-looking dolls, as well as some disabled ones, as all the dolls were 'able-bodied'. It is lunacy, and it is bullying.

So we set our children this kind of example when they are at their most impressionable – it's no surprise that so many of them turn into bullies themselves. And it's easy for them to find a target. We've all got something – we're fat, or we've got freckles, or we've got big ears, or we've got a big nose or, in the case of Wayne Rooney, we've got all of the above (sorry, Wayne, no bullying intended!) – so we're all vulnerable to it.

So how should we deal with this ever-increasing problem? I'm a firm believer that you can measure the quality of a school by its policy on bullying – it's astounding how many parents find that the only solution to the problem is to move into another borough in order to get their bullied child into a different school. In some cases, the school is even a fee-paying one, so the parents have the pleasure of actually paying for their children to undergo this shameful treatment. And the truth is that, to a certain extent, the only thing a bully understands is a taste of his own medicine. This doesn't mean that you have to go around slapping him or her around the head, but it does mean that teachers should be in a position to exert some sort of discipline if they are going to be able to monitor the bully and show them a path out of it. There's no point sitting them down for a cup of tea and a biscuit and asking them nicely if they'll stop doing it – they'll just laugh in your face, or at the very least behind your back. They need to be censured and punished; they need to have privileges denied them; it needs to be made clear that their behaviour won't be tolerated.

If our teachers aren't allowed a free hand to do this, without fear of being punished themselves, then all that will happen is that little bullies will grow up to be big bullies. Who knows, they might even end up as Prime Minister...

Having it all, and why you can't — even if you're Germaine Greer

I'd like to tell you a story. Are you sitting comfortably? Then I'll begin.

It's an everyday story of boy meets girl. They are both in their early twenties, and the sparks are there. He ticks all the right boxes: he's good-looking, he makes her laugh, everything's hunky-dory between the sheets, her mum likes him and, most importantly of all, he'd make a great dad. He'd like to settle down, and this is where the problem lies. She's not ready for all that, and for the very best of reasons. I'm building my career, she tells herself. I'm going places. If I work hard, I could be area manager in a couple of years, and then who knows? I certainly don't want to think about having children just yet – plenty of time for that when I've done everything I want to do.

So, despite the fact that it's a marriage made in heaven – or at least it could be – boy goes off and finds himself someone else who is as keen as he is to start a family. Meanwhile, girl puts her head down, works hard and sure enough she becomes area manager. She's a high-flyer and a go-getter, but suddenly she stops to take stock and she realises she's approaching her mid-thirties. Right, she thinks, now's the time. I've been at the company for ten years, I'll get great maternity pay, I've achieved a certain level that means I can come back or even act as a consultant. Her biological clock is not just ticking, it started ringing ages ago and, by now, it's fallen over and dropped off the bedside table. So she starts to look around.

But now she runs into a problem: the only blokes she can find are either (a) happily married, (b) unhappily married but not willing to leave the wife, or (c) very, very ugly. So she hangs around in wine bars with other thirtysomething single women, drinking Chardonnay in Bridget Jones quantities, being grumpy and moaning about how much they hate men. (And the more they drink, the more the deny that they are drunk. Nick Ferrari's Law of Drunkenness: the more someone denies that they are drunk, the drunker they are. And whenever anybody says, 'I'm not saying this because I've had a drink,' beware: they're *only* saying it because they've had a drink.)

Well, there's nothing more unattractive to a bloke than a bunch of half-pissed women being miserable and saying how much they despise every man that ever walked the earth: if a half-decent catch does happen to come along, he's going to run a mile – probably breaking the world record as he does so...

At this stage, before I alienate my entire female readership and have you all come round to attack my house, I'll concede that I'm half-joking. But only half. Women, it seems to me, have been sold an impossible dream by the likes of Germaine Greer. Women *cannot* have it all, and to suggest that they can is irresponsible.

Nor can men, of course. I don't want to suggest that I don't feel lucky to be a bloke, or that I don't have enormous sympathy for the predicament of women in the modern world, but I nevertheless envy them in some ways. I envy them that they have the sensation of carrying a child; I envy the bond that must exist between a mother and the child they have carried. I am incredibly fortunate to have the brilliant relationship I have with my two sons, but still ... to have carried them for nine months. To bear a child must be the biggest privilege a human being can have. But there it is. And it's a fact of life that the bulk of the work of raising a child in its early infancy is down to the mother: it might not be how we want it to be, but that's how it is, and it's down to biology, not chauvinism.

We often have this conversation on the radio, and I frequently receive calls from married working mums who say that if they didn't work, they couldn't meet the bills. Well, OK – there are always going to be people for whom this is true, and these are people who really do genuinely have the bad end of the deal. But, in many cases, you can certainly make the argument that perhaps you don't really *need* three holidays a year – perhaps you won't be able to go skiing this Christmas after all. It's not right, but it's a fact of life: if you want children and you stop work, you'll have to go without something.

It would be easier, I think, if there wasn't such a terrible stigma attached to the word 'housewife'. You see it all the time. If you chat to people at a party, they will tell you at the drop of a hat if they're a designer, or an author, or an airline pilot, or (heaven forbid) a lawyer, but if they look after their children, they will always say, 'Oh, I'm *just* a housewife.' That is absolutely terrible. Why 'just'? What you are doing is raising secure children who are the next generation of designers, authors, airline pilots, lawyers and, yes, housewives. What more important – and difficult – work could there be? But you've been sold the impossible dream – you think you should be able to do all this *and* be executive chairman of ICI. It puts you in a terrible dilemma.

And families are not helped by the government. Clearly nobody gets married and has children in order to save money – they wouldn't have a very sound financial head on their shoulders if they did – but, nevertheless, there used to be certain tax incentives and benefits that would accrue if you were married, and I think that is wholly appropriate. Children benefit from being raised within the confines of a happy marriage. Now, obviously, if you have children and you are not married, it doesn't mean it's going to be a disaster, but there doesn't seem to be any doubt among right-thinking people that in a perfect world Mummy and Daddy will get on very well and their children will benefit enormously from that relationship. The government's role should be to support that. Obviously nobody is saying that if you don't manage to achieve this we're going to pelt you with rotten eggs in the street – we're not going to put you in the stocks because you're a single mum – and obviously it's our duty to look after everyone equally. But why should we not be able to encourage people down this path by rewarding them if they manage to achieve it?

Unfortunately, it seems to be heading in the other direction at the moment. Gay couples have many of the same rights as married couples. Absolutely fine; but some councils fall over themselves to ensure that gay couples get special consideration when it comes to fostering and adoption. How can that be right? I can understand that a gay couple can be a perfect family unit and will do a great job of raising children, but why on earth should their rights of becoming adoptive parents be given precedence over those of a conventional married couple?

So now, it seems that not only does being a housewife have a terrible stigma, being married does, too. 'Oh dear,' people seem to say. 'How very old fashioned. Why are you married? Why aren't you just partners?' No wonder married women feel under pressure to prove themselves. No wonder they try to have it all...

A night out in London

'I'm going up west.' It used to be a statement almost as glamorous as saying, 'I'm flying club class to Monte Carlo, where I intend to drink only the finest Krug as I clean up at the blackjack tables.' Or, 'The chauffeur was having trouble grooming the mink coverings on the second Jag, so one of them had to go, unfortunately for him.'

No matter that you were only going to the *Talk of the Town* to see Cilla Black, a night out in London had a real ring to it. It was something to look forward to. It was special.

Not any more. Why? Because your evening's ruined before you even manage to settle down to your first gin and tonic in the theatre bar.

Getting into London in the evening is a bit like that scene at the beginning of *Indiana Jones and the Raiders of the Lost Ark* – a sequence of increasingly fearsome challenges that can only be overcome using guile, experience and a not-inconsequential amount of good luck. Clearly cycling is not an option for normal, level-headed people with half a brain, so let's say you decide to incur the wrath of Ken Livingstone and drive. Sod's law dictates that you'll arrive on the edge of the congestion charge zone just before half past six, so you have an option: do you get mugged for the eight quid it's going to cost you to beat the traffic into the zone; or do you do what everybody else is doing and park up in a side street to listen to the radio or read the paper until six thirty and one second, at which stage you will need to join the mad scramble. Seeing the backlog of cars zoom into the congestion zone at half past six is a bit like watching a herd of crazed wildebeest charge across the African savannah on a David Attenborough wildlife programme. Indeed, I can imagine the quietly spoken voiceover: 'And now, using the inbuilt clock nature has so generously bestowed upon him, the lesser spotted commuter appears as if from nowhere, safe in the knowledge that he is free from his two most feared predators: the traffic warden and the camera. Crazed with impatience and thirst, he joins with his herd-mates and, in a matter of a few startling seconds, a thundering stampede ensues. Beware anyone who finds themselves in the path of these speeding beasts as they embark upon yet another hurdle in their constant daily struggle: the search for a parking spot sufficiently close to their preferred watering hole.'

Hollywood has a lot to answer for, but none of their sins is so great as the false expectations they have instilled in the average city dweller regarding the parking of one's car. I'm sure you know what I'm talking about: those movies when an impossibly chiselled Tom Cruise has arranged to meet an unspeakably beautiful Uma Thurman in an unreasonably glamorous restaurant. Why is it that whenever *he* wants to park, there's *always* a parking spot right outside? I know from experience that it's not like that in LA, but it's even less likely in London. In fact, I have noticed that there is an incredible law of nature at work here: Ferrari's

Law of Parking/Climate Relativity states that the colder it is, the further you will have to park from your desired destination. Let's say you want to go to a restaurant on Bond Street. If it's cold enough to freeze the appendages off a brass monkey, you'll probably have to park somewhere on the outskirts of Neasden. If it's reasonably balmy you might, if you're lucky, get within half a mile, but it would have to be hot enough to make St Lucia look like St Albans if you want to park right outside your destination. Another reason, then, to support the onset of global warming.

Ah! But what have you forgotten to do? That's right – you haven't checked the parking restrictions, have you? So as you waddle back from dinner, you turn into the street in which you parked to see the stomach-churning sight of a yellow clamp adorning one of your wheels.

Clamping, for me, is one of the most infuriatingly daft inventions of modern times. Your car's in the way, we need a thoroughfare of traffic, so what shall we do? We'll clamp the bugger. That way, when you come back to your car that is supposedly in a prime spot and holding everyone up, we'll make sure that you won't be able to move it until you've paid a few hundred quid and sat in the car for another three hours or so while you wait for the unclamping van to toddle along. By the time it does, you are ready to kill. You can't condone it, but you can see why it is that these guys get assaulted. They get out of their van (which they've stopped in the middle of the street, so holding up more traffic), their knuckles dragging so low to the ground that they look the closest to Neanderthal man you'll see this side of the missing link. Watching motorists having a bit of argy-bargy with these guys has become London's best spectator sport: you get the frisson of the argument without the dubious outcome of an actual fight (no one in their right minds would take these Mike Tyson body doubles on…).

Alternatively you could try taking public transport. Let me tell you about the last time I did that.

The occasion was a newspaper's Christmas party. Now, it is not unheard of for a glass or two of wine to be consumed at these occasions and so, deciding that I would join in the fun, I elected not to drive but to take the train from my local railway station. I spruced myself up and dug out a fairly smart business suit and started walking towards the station. Out of the blue a kid walks up to me. 'Spare some change?' he asked.

'I'm sorry, mate,' I told him, 'I don't have any.'

I had hardly finished my sentence before he threw half a bottle of lemonade all over my suit. In that moment, I felt a sensation that I have thankfully never encountered before or since: sympathy for John Prescott. It may not have been an egg that was hurled at me, and I may not have been in front of the television cameras, but my urge to retaliate was just as strong. Fortunately I managed to fight the urge, but the net result was that I found myself sitting on a rather grimy train, the sickly sweet odour of lemonade emanating from uncomfortably damp trousers.

Ever the optimist, I tried to cheer myself up. At least I'd managed to find one of the few seats that hadn't been adorned with bloody great globules of chewing gum; at least the smell of lemonade was overpowering the slightly more unpleasant whiff of stale urine that was pervading the carriage. Maybe I should just look out of the window and watch the world go by…

As I did so, I made a mental note to write a letter to the managing director of Hornby. As you probably know, toy train manufacturers supply a wide range of accessories for their train sets: tunnels, signals, stations, level crossings. You name it, if it appears on a railway track or by the sidings, Hornby has done it in miniature.

With one exception: miniature piles of crap. You know the stuff – rubble, graffitied walls, old oil drums – the kind of thing that looks as if it's been imported in bulk from war-torn Baghdad. This is the stuff that their creative department need to turn their attention to if they are successfully to recreate the special ambience of the twenty-first-century British railway.

Finally my train arrived in central London and I made my way to the underground. The tube journey was predictably awful, but made only slightly better because the rest of the passengers on the tube gave my sodden trousers as wide a berth as the overcrowded carriage would allow.

So that's your choice for a night out in London. It's not much of a choice, is it? Personally, I'd rather stay at home and watch the telly. Speaking of which...

"No qualifications, no interests or hobbies and limited vocabulary. We'll get you on Big Brother..."

Big Brother might be watching me, but I'm certainly not watching him...

It is the mark of a civilised country that we should have developed ever more imaginative and piquant ways of wasting our time.

Take cricket, for example. How else could we justify parking our bum on the couch for five days solid, or whittling away valuable office time watching live news feeds of the latest Test score when we should be putting the finishing touches to that presentation? It is the very height of sophistication, the thing that separates us from the animals: dogs must make do with chasing their tails to relieve their boredom, whereas we can get away with conversations like this:

'Cor, I'm knackered, mate.'

'Really? What have you been up to today?'

'Watching the cricket.'

What we mean, of course, is that we did absolutely nothing; but we have an excuse.

There are countless other fabulous time-wasting pursuits we have invented. Crossword puzzles. Going for a drink. Having a lie-in. Trying to get through to a real human at a call centre. Each one of them is a mark of our civilised superiority.

But we have to draw the line somewhere. And that line should be drawn straight through the employment contracts of the television executives who have filled our TVs with the mind-numbing, licence-fee-wasting dross that is 'reality television'. This sorry little band of programmes seems to have bred at a rate that would make the friskiest rabbit feel like he was firing blanks. Each new reality TV show seems to spawn a couple of weakling offspring, each more ridiculous, strained and embarrassing to those involved than the last. We've had live autopsies, live celebrity snogging, we've had young people being humiliated, old people being humiliated. Where it will end I do not know: I'm tempted to nip in to Channel 4 right now and pitch Live Celebrity Autopsy but, on reflection, I don't think I want to sow the seeds of that particular notion for fear that I might be asked to appear on it.

The crowning turd in the toilet of reality TV, of course, is *Big Brother*. Clearly the producers go out of their way to find the most nauseating ragbag of fame-hungry, exhibitionist, moronic layabouts they can put their hands on in the hope that their self-serving antics will somehow capture the attention of the poor audience, starved into watching it by the fact that this pernicious programme is an ever-present feature of the summer schedules.

But my main bugbear with *Big Brother* is not the people I'm forced to watch on it: it's the fact that nothing ever, *ever* happens. Indeed, that seems to be the whole point of the operation: put a bunch of people with small brains and big egos into a house together and, with the exception of a few rather feeble 'tasks', leave them to do nothing. Pointless people doing sod all: it doesn't sound like a winner to me. I came home one evening to find the airwaves full of live 'action' from the *Big Brother* house.

Unfortunately, the housemates had all gone to bed, so the only action we saw was everyone lying under their duvets snoring, occasionally cut with an image of an empty corridor. This took up a good chunk of programming time: am I the only one who thinks we're being conned?

To say it's stultifying is a massive understatement. I know not a *lot* happens in cricket, but at least there's a structure to the thing, and a score, and a bit of excitement. At the very least you can watch the Barmy Army get slowly sozzled as the day progresses and turn a shocking and potentially lethal shade of pink. I would have to be very desperate indeed to allot some of those precious hours set aside for time-wasting to watching *Big Brother*, where people who *can't* do anything sit around *not* doing anything.

And as if it weren't enough that we have to endure watching these ghastly people during the substantial amount of time that *Big Brother* is on TV, suddenly a select handful of them seem insistent on prostituting themselves in whatever sordid way they see fit in order to maintain the scant level of celebrity that they have so far achieved. In the past, of course, celebrity really meant something. It meant you had talent and dedication, it meant you were not afraid of hard work and paying your dues in order to be top of your game. As I write this, the nation is still mourning the passing of Ronnie Barker: he achieved his celebrity through genuine brilliance and good, old-fashioned elbow grease. But now, our appetite for celebrity has grown so large that they need to be manufactured on an almost week-by-week basis, and *Big Brother* is the archetypal celebrity-making machine. Of course, none of these people have anything to back up their celebrity – there are no dedicated musicians or actors or writers or artists – but that's not why they're there. It would be too much like hard work, wouldn't it?

The net result is that we do not seem to be able to rid ourselves of the sight (and more distressingly the sound) of Jade Goody. I don't know this young woman – she is no doubt absolutely lovely – but let's be honest: she's only famous for being a bit thick, and I'm really not sure that's a good enough reason for her to be on my television all the time.

So when reality TV turns on, I turn off. With

one exception. The glorious sight of assorted B-listers humiliating themselves by undergoing the most revolting challenges imaginable is just too tempting for me to resist, so I am an avid viewer of *I'm a Celebrity, Get Me Out of Here!* Jordan dropping hairy spiders down her bra? That's entertainment! Janet Street Porter eating witchetty grubs? Beats *Coronation Street* any day of the week. And to top it all, if they fail, their fellow contestants don't eat. It's elemental stuff. If I had my way, they'd introduce a bit more of this draconian attitude into the *Big Brother* house. Starve them. Torture them. Or even – and I might be going a bit too far here – stop them from ever appearing on television again if they don't start being a bit more entertaining.

Until that happens, I'm sticking to the cricket.

America? China? Nah . . . it's all happening in Tescoland

Consider, if you will, a day in the life of the average Albanian peasant.

It's no picnic, let me tell you. It's still a land of horses and carts. People are forced to live near the toxic-waste sites because they can't afford to live anywhere else. The most exciting thing that happens in Albania is when a Norman Wisdom film comes on the television. Now, I like Norman Wisdom as much as the next man, but the idea that all I had to look forward to was *A Stitch in Time* being shown at eight o'clock tonight is not something that gets me itching to pack my bags and jet off to Tirana. No, the truth is that Albania's not much fun.

I have a simple way to rectify all this. It might not be entirely popular with the current Albanian administration, and I concede that it's maverick, but it will certainly turn the place around.

Think of McDonald's. It's a multinational, global brand. It doesn't matter if you're in New York or New Malden, you know exactly what you are going to get when you walk into a McDonald's. They have successfully managed to take their product to the four corners of the earth and keep it completely true to their global strategy. You know the quality of food that you're going to get, you know you can feed your family for under fifteen quid and, despite what people say, you know that you're not going to get food poisoning! The Big Mac you buy in Birmingham is going to be exactly the same as the Big Mac you buy in Beijing. It might sound like a small point, but actually that's quite a feat. What it represents is commercial and administrative brilliance at its very best.

Or take Tesco. Of every eight pounds we spend in the high street, one of those pounds is spent in Tesco. One in eight – it's really something. I know that if I go into a Tesco in Aberdeen, I'm going to get exactly the same quality as if I go into Tesco in Anglesey or Ashford. They can move all this food around the country, market it and sell it, and become one of the most successful companies in Britain. This is astonishing. Tesco is clearly run by some of the most brilliant people in the country.

Unfortunately, because there is a certain sector of this country who like to piss on everyone's chips, Tesco's brilliance really does not get acknowledged like it ought to. When they hear that a company has been fabulously successful, they start clamouring that there should be a windfall tax. Why? Why on earth should we penalise people for being successful? It's like telling Chelsea they have to go down to ten men because they've been scoring too many goals. Just because Tesco have managed to source the cheapest baked beans, just because they've had great advertising campaigns with Prunella Scales wandering up and down and buying cakes every Christmas, just because everybody shops there and their products are very, very good – why should they have to pay more tax than someone else who does the same job only not as well?

I would do things quite differently.

The big hitters in big business are economic and logistical geniuses. It strikes me that they have proved themselves to be competent of taking on even bigger things.

So I would give them Albania, and let them call it Tescoland.

And I'd give other failing countries to other successful big businesses, too. McDonald's can have Togo and Microsoft can have Bangladesh. The CEOs can become presidents, and if they apply their awe-inspiring business skills to the running of the administrations, they'll soon get those places back on their feet again. We won't be able to rest on our laurels, content in the knowledge that we're the fourth-biggest economy in the world. You mark my words, before long they'll have Tescoland snapping at our heels. Look out, America; mind your back, China; President Gates of Microsoftland is going to put you in your place.

We could use the same principle to bring us benefits at home, too. In a perfect world, the people who work for companies like Tesco and Burger King would be attracted towards working in government and on behalf of our public services. It doesn't happen that way, of course, because, broadly speaking, the private sector pays more money than the public sector. This means that all the decent people go and work for McDonald's, and Kodak, and Disney, and BP, and Shell; it's the ones who are left who end up working for the National Health Service, and the Department of Education, and the Ministry of Defence. Billions of pounds are pumped into the NHS every year, and I for one would feel more confident if it were managed by someone who is king of the hill, not bottom of the heap.

So we need a rethink, and I am of the opinion that what we do for Albania we can do for the NHS. Let's give it to Waitrose. They can't make a worse job of it than the current lot. 'Look,' we can tell them, 'you've had a fantastic year. Here's the NHS. Look after it, and if you do well – *if* you do well, mind, we're not promising anything – we might give you schools next year.' That way we'll have all the most brilliant people in the country looking after all the most important organisations we have. They'd get Jamie Oliver to advertise what a pukka idea it is to work hard at your geography homework. They could encourage people into the teaching profession by offering them cheap supermarket booze (I've never met a teacher yet whose eyes didn't light up at the prospect of a gin and tonic). They can even flog some of their marvellous free-range chickens to the hospital canteens – the nationwide loathing for hospital food will be wiped out overnight. And that's got to be a splendid idea, hasn't it?

Giving Auntie a kick up the jacksie

If you are a BBC executive, or a senior commissioning editor, or you think that the BBC is a bastion of everything that makes this country great, might I delicately suggest that you stop reading. Now.

It's no secret that I am a long-standing critic of the BBC. Time and again there are myriad programmes about the BBC on television – is the licence fee good value for money, should it be scrapped, is the programming what it might be, is it dumbing down – and more often than not I am wheeled on to ITV News or Sky to give my views. Most curiously of all, however, given that those views are less than favourable, I am also wheeled on to discussions on the BBC.

It's taken me a while to work out why this should be so, but I think I've finally cracked it. The BBC have an innate love of self-flagellation. The more I criticise them, the more they ask me back. It's the only place in the world where this happens. Any ordinary, sensible, private company would do exactly the opposite. If I wandered around telling all and sundry that I thought the *Sun* was a load of absolute rubbish, the newspaper's executives would soon enough say, 'Right, I've had quite enough of that fat bugger wandering around slagging us off. I never want to see Nick Ferrari's ugly mug in this paper ever again.' And that would be that. But the BBC are the exact opposite. They like being criticised, and they don't want anybody to believe that they can't take it. So instead of giving me the cold shoulder, they say, 'Oh, bloody hell, I saw that Nick Ferrari on ITV last night and he was giving us a right kick up the jacksie. We'd better have him on again...'

So, in the interest of boosting my future employment prospects at the Corporation, allow me to explain in minute detail just what I think is wrong with the BBC.

We now have a couple of toll roads in this

country – you pay a few quid in order to use them. Clearly, however, you don't pay any money if you want to use the other roads. So, stay off the toll roads and you don't pay a fee. It's not a bad analogy for the TV. What if you were to tell the government that you would never watch any BBC channels? Ask them to take them away. And you won't listen to any BBC radio either. You'll be more than adequately served by ITV, Sky, local radio – whatever else it is you want to listen to, just not the BBC. Why on earth would you still have to pay the toll that the licence fee essentially is in order to be able to do this? It is clearly, and fundamentally, wrong.

And what does the licence fee get spent on? I certainly wouldn't say that much of it goes on quality programming. Certainly a fair old chunk goes on sending BBC executives on corporate bonding sessions in posh country hotels that cost thousands of pounds a night. And I can't imagine how many hundreds of thousands go on those ridiculous rebranding exercises they do from time to time. You know the things I mean: those ridiculous links involving a bunch of samba dancers waving a load of red silk in the air, or those Zen-monk types practising their transcendental meditation, or some geezer swinging down from a bloody great rope. They're all very pretty to look at, I suppose, but hardly a fabulous use of the licence-payers' money. If they were a bit more entertaining it would be a different matter – if it were a fat bloke like me swinging down from the rope, that would be worth watching! – but, as it is, it is a total waste of money.

So how else would we fund programming on the BBC if we didn't have the licence fee. Obviously, as many people will tell you, we can't have advertising or sponsorship. Well, why on earth not? Why does it matter if at the start of *EastEnders* someone says, '*EastEnders* is brought to you by Ariel Automatic'? What's going to happen? Is the world suddenly going to end? Will there be rioting in the streets? Will our television sets explode? So *EastEnders* is brought to me by Ariel Automatic. Fine. I don't have a problem with that.

In fact, I'd go a step further. Let's have a bit more product placement. Picture it: Huw Edwards is reading the news, and the camera cuts from Kate Adie in the field or John

Simpson liberating Kabul to the smooth Welshman picking up a steaming mug of coffee and saying, 'Well, that's very interesting, John. Now, I just need a quick cup of Maxwell House – freeze dried to taste as good as fresh! Aaaahhh, that's better.' Even if everyone then goes out and buys Maxwell House instead of Nescafé, is it really going to corrupt the morals of a nation? I think not. The viewers and listeners, you see, are far, far, smarter than any of these watchdog bodies give them credit for…

But the proof of the pudding, they say, is in the eating: what we're really concerned about is the quality of the material on the telly. So, as I write this, I am looking at the schedule for tonight on the BBC. This evening's programmes include *Cash in the Attic* and something called *Car Booty*. But worst of all, and I don't quite know how to break this to you, if I want to sit in front of the gogglebox tonight and make the most of my licence fee money, I'm going to have to put up with the sight and sound of … I can hardly say it … *Bill Oddie*.

Make me Prime Minister and I promise you two things: I'll give you your licence fee money back *and* I'll ban Bill Oddie.

Help! Is there an aromatherapist in the house?

I want to believe in alternative medicine. I really do. How marvellous it would be if we could knock up a mixture of dock leaves and goat's urine to find a failsafe cure for haemorrhoids. What a boon to mankind it would be if we could cure the common cold with a concoction of ladybird spittle and onion leaves. And fair do's to Prince Charles for wandering around telling us that if we chew on a piece of tree bark we will cure our rheumatism in a flash: he obviously wants to believe it just as much as I do.

But there's a small problem with the vast majority of alternative medicine. It's a little thing, but it seems to have been overlooked by almost everyone who subscribes to it.

It's a load of utter baloney.

OK, maybe I'd better qualify that a bit. I'll reluctantly concede that there *might* be a place for *some* of the alternative therapies that we are force-fed in the Sunday supplements week in, week out. But my real gripe is with all these new-age, tree-hugging, knitted-Peruvian-hat-wearing hippies who tell us that we should reject modern medicine in favour of 'natural' alternatives. You know the sort: if you've got a migraine they'll tell you to rub the back of your neck instead of reaching for the Nurofen. God forbid they ever have any kind of serious medical problem, but if they did there is a mischievous part of me that can't help wishing that they would be given a taste of their own alternative medicine.

Imagine the scene. One of these fellows is knocked off his bike on the way to the organic health-food shop to buy some hemp oil for his nut roast and stock up on fair-trade Ginkgo Balboa, and he breaks his leg. He gets wheeled off to Casualty. 'Ah,' says the duty doctor, 'we've got you down as an alternative-health practitioner.'

'Yes, yes, I am.'

'OK, well we've got some stinging nettles

growing out the back. If I get those, and mix them up with a bit of crushed dandelion to make a soothing poultice, how does that sound?'

The reality is, of course, that he'd give his entire collection of Eritrean wall rugs for an anaesthetic and some pain killers, and he'll want them to work now!

The trouble with alternative therapies is that they are so open to conmen, quackery and snake-oil merchants. I swear that the display of alternative medicines at my local chemist is bigger than the display of traditional medicines. But I know that if I've got – and I'm sorry to inflict this image upon you – an appalling case of diarrhoea, I'm going to want the most potent drug available to man. I don't care if, to bring this drug to me, thousands of cuddly rabbits have had bugs and nasties injected into them – as long as it's going to make me close up like a safe, that's OK in my books. I'm certainly not going to think, Hmmm, ground eggshells, a little bit of nutmeg, smear that on my lower regions and Bob's your uncle. I want drugs and I want them to work in seconds.

It's galling to think that so many people are so down on the amazing advances modern medicine has achieved. An unfortunate side-effect of these advances has been the necessity for certain treatments to be tested on animals. But it is just that: a necessity. Vivisection works and, thanks to animal testing, huge advances have been made and drugs have been introduced safely that have minimised pain for those poor souls suffering such complaints as diverse as Parkinson's disease and multiple sclerosis. That's not to say it shouldn't be controlled – obviously it is completely repugnant that animal testing should be used for cosmetics. This happens and it is ridiculous and wrong. But where it might lead to a medical advance – and I use the word 'might' advisedly, as the very nature of medical research is that scientists are generally groping in the dark for new medicines – and as long as it is done as humanely as can be and no glee or pleasure is taken from the animal's suffering and it is put out of its misery if that is the best thing to do, then it is as clear as night follows day that vivisection and other forms of animal testing have to stay.

The truth is that medical science has advanced at such a rate that the NHS has struggled to keep up with it in financial terms. We now have so many drugs available to us, to cure so many different illnesses, that the NHS simply cannot afford to supply all these drugs to everybody that wants them. We are left with the shameful travesty of the postcode lottery, which dictates that the care you are likely to receive if you have a serious illness is directly related to the wealth of the borough in which you live. This is clearly appalling, but is the obvious outcome of the NHS the way it is run at the moment.

So let's have some tough talking. Let's come out and say it. Quite plainly, the NHS as we currently expect it to function cannot work.

When it was initially set up in 1948, the thinking was that it would make us healthier and, as a result, we would have to use it less. In those days it was a fabulous benefit, but successive generations have come to see it as their birthright. We see our NI contributions come out of our pay cheque and we think, Well, I pay for the health service, so I expect it to be there for me. The reality, however, is that we live in a country where we all live a lot longer and diseases that would have wiped us out even forty years ago can be completely contained and treated. So, while it's perfectly true that people *should* have access to the drugs they need, we have to come to terms with the fact that the NHS is a finite resource.

Any government or potential government that wants to gain power or increase its popularity will say that they will pump more money into the NHS; what none of them will say, because it is political suicide, is that it needs to be scrapped as it currently exists.

Of course we need to have some sort of emergency service, so that if anybody gets knocked down by a bus there is provision for them, but we really ought to be looking at something much more along the lines of the Australian model. Under that system, the state provides you with a sum of money to see your doctor, but you may have to wait a few days. However, you can top that money up from your own pocket and see someone that day. Of course, many people will argue that doing that puts the poor at a terrible disadvantage, and to some extent that is true. But it is a fact of life that the poor will always be with us, and there will always be a discrepancy in what they can afford when compared with those who are better off. And, in any case, they well be aided, because the pressure on the health system will be relieved by those who can afford to pay a little extra.

It will never happen, of course. No matter that this country has the distinction of an entry in the *Guinness Book of Records* for the longest time an elderly person has spent on a trolley in a hospital ward. It is approaching seventy-two hours.

It's enough to make you feel nauseous. Pass the royal jelly.

On second thoughts, make it a pack of Setler's Tums.

How do we put up with Ken? And how does he put up with me?

Please don't take this personally Ken, but I'm afraid London does not need you.

What we have in Ken Livingstone is a perfect example of classic British compromise. We're very good at compromise, us Brits – I think it must spring from the days when we ran an empire and had to hone our diplomatic skills extremely finely – but it's not always a good thing, and it certainly isn't when it comes to the position of Mayor of London. If you go to other cities, like New York or Tokyo, the mayor has power, *real* power (cue diabolical laughing and rubbing of hands in glee). He or she drives the whole equation: not only are they in charge of the funding as well as running all the education and the policing, they are also fully in charge of transport and can make a real difference. What the British have done in London, as only the British can do, is to appoint a democratically elected mayor, but to decline to give him all the powers he wants. So, instead of him being able to get hold of the city and do what he really wants to do, he has to dance around the edges, tweaking this, adjusting that, but not really able to do very much at all. He's really neither one thing nor the other.

So far so useless. But do you know what? I'm pleased it's this way round, and I daily thank God that Ken Livingstone doesn't have any more powers. Can you imagine the state we'd be in if – as is the case in New York – the mayor was in a position to raise taxes? Ken is hardly known for his tax-reduction policies, and he taxes us enough with the congestion charge as it is. Giving him total control over the purse strings of London is absolutely unthinkable.

It's also a quite astonishing waste of time and resources. Think of City Hall. I can't imagine how much it must cost to keep that place going. There's no denying that it is aesthetically sensational, but we're all paying for it. Why on earth couldn't they just move into any one of the office spaces you see around the capital that's just standing there idle waiting for the squatters and the drug addicts to move in? Why are we spending millions on this building when we quite clearly don't need it?

What's more, it is very interesting to note that only two out of every ten Londoners actually voted for Ken Livingstone. The rest either voted for other people or – in the vast majority of cases – didn't vote at all. They just couldn't be motivated. And of those that voted for him, half of them only did so because they thought it would be a jolly good wheeze to stick two fingers up to Blair. The two are not exactly bosom buddies, and we're a bit like that in London!

Ken and I have, shall we say, a slightly chequered history. When he once refused to answer my telephone calls regarding a particular issue, I made an appeal on the radio. I gave out his office number – *not* his home number – and I said to my listeners, 'Look, I'm sorry to have to ask you to do this, and I'm sorry it's going to cost you money to make the call, but this guy won't answer my calls on behalf of all you Londoners that have given me your support, and I think it's bloody rude. So if you could all phone his office and ask why not, I'd appreciate it.' Needless to say the switchboard was jammed and Red Ken went even redder in the face with anger. He accused me of doing all sorts of things – breaking this code, breaking that code – and he wrote to everybody he could think of (my bosses, my agent, broadcasting authorities) trying to get me fired. For ages he wouldn't have any contact with me.

The trouble is that he's actually quite a charismatic bloke these days, and has mellowed a bit by becoming a father late in life. It was much easier in Mrs Thatcher's day, when you could just put him in a corner and say, Red Ken, barking mad, loves the IRA, don't go near him. Nowadays he's altogether more cuddly. And our relationship has improved. He often comes on the show, so I get to talk to him at length. Now it's much easier to be mean to somebody if you're Jeremy Paxman or John Humphries. On their shows the willing victim is wheeled on, the grand inquisitor rips the crap out of them, and then they're wheeled off again. It doesn't work like that with me. If the mayor is with me for, say, an hour, we have to sit together through the

news, through the travel, through the weather –
by the end of it you've had quite a considerable
amount of time just chatting to him one to one
without anybody else listening and, of course,
two reasonable people are going to develop
some sort of rapport. The truth is that we now
get on quite well. I don't regret it, but really our
relationship was better when it was more
combative and I was in a position where I had to
chit-chat with him occasionally.

So underneath it all he's not a bad bloke, and
he does have a sense of humour. When I went
with one of my sons to City Hall to pick up the
kit I wore when I carried the Olympic torch
through London, we bumped into each other.
'You're not running with the torch, are you?' he
asked me, understandably incredulous.

'Well,' I told him, 'I criticised our chances of
getting the Olympics because I don't think we
could organise a piss-up in a brewery, but I'm
perfectly happy to run my fat arse through
London so we can all have a good laugh. Why
don't you do the same?'

Ken just laughed then turned to my son.
'How do you put up with him?' he asked.

Which is a very good question, of course…

If in doubt, ask Sid

I have a new candidate for Prime Minister. His name is Sid.

Sid has no background in politics. Come to think of it, I don't reckon he's even particularly *interested* in politics. He's not especially good looking, charming or well spoken, and he certainly doesn't have the Machiavellian instinct that seems to be essential to modern-day politicians. He probably wouldn't instantly appeal to the grass-roots members of any particular party and the chances of him winning an election are frankly nil. He's about ninety – hardly in his prime. Sid wouldn't know a quango if it fell on him and if you asked him what he thought of the latest white paper, he'd probably advise you to go for the more expensive stuff if you want to avoid getting air bubbles on your living-room wall.

Sid, you see, is a member of staff at my local B&Q. Now, I know this might not make him sound like an obvious candidate for political greatness, but hear me out.

Sid knows everything. I've never had a problem he couldn't solve. (Actually, there was one problem he'd have had difficulty with, but the antibiotics soon sorted that out.) His knowledge is startling. To date, thanks to Sid's impeccable advice, I've repaired three lawnmowers and a hedge-trimmer, redone my guttering, redone my glazing, sorted out my electrics, done the plumbing and even tried my hand at a bit of plastering. No matter how daunting the job, I approach the unflappable Sid and he comes up with a sure-fire solution. I'm fully convinced that if I were to catch him when he's not too busy on a quiet Tuesday afternoon and say, 'Look, Sid, I've got a real problem. This whole business of world poverty is really getting me down. What do you think I should do about it?', he'd soon come up with a foolproof way of cancelling world debt and bringing clean drinking water to the dying masses. 'What you want, Nick old son, is a nice long piece of copper piping and a good quality pressure valve. I think we've got some on isle nine.'

If Sid were Prime Minister, he wouldn't have any difficulty whatsoever filling up all those tricky ministerial posts. His cabinet would be full of elderly workers in DIY stores. Do you think that sounds like a stupid idea? Well, here's a tip. Next time you go to *your* local DIY store, look out for the oldest member of staff you can find. He will undoubtedly be the wisest. What you don't want is some shaven-headed youth who is only there because he's on some work in the community project, and who can't hear what you're asking him anyway because one ear is stuffed full of an iPod headphone blaring the latest horrific sounds from whatever ghastly band he likes to listen to. Don't even think of going up to him and saying, 'Excuse me, mate, I don't suppose you happen to have a brass lug screw for an original Victorian mortice-style lock, do you?' You might just as well be speaking to him in Dutch and the only response you'll get is a look such as you might expect if you had just asked to sleep with his girlfriend.

No, you want the old boys. They'll sort you out in the blink of an eye. They've done it all, and there's nothing they haven't seen. That's why I think we should forget these young political whippersnappers and leave the running of the country to the Sids of the world. Northern Ireland Minister? Ray from plumbing. Anyone who can deal with those argumentative plumbers with such consummate skill has to be a world-class negotiator. Foreign Secretary? Well, Bill in electrics can translate even the most perplexing technical mumbo-jumbo into straightforward English, so he'll be the man for that job.

Under Sid's administration, there is no doubt that productivity will go up. He's so encouraging that he's even had me deciding to do jobs that I don't even really need to do – and I don't just mean the small stuff, either. In fact, small jobs don't hold much interest for me any more. I can't be bothered with painting, for a start, because it's just so boring. If I were to come round and paint your house, you'd just have to accept that the walls are going to be the same colour as the skirting board – I simply can't be bothered with all those namby-pamby details. No, what I like is the big jobs, the manly jobs. Re-roofing the garage. Rendering the outside walls. And I'm never happier than when I'm wearing the big old tool belt Sid told me to buy. He's taught me respect for my tools and he's right: you can always trust a bloke who loves his screwdriver and nothing makes you feel more like a man than a bloody great set of spanners.

And thanks to Sid, I've been passing my love of DIY on to my sons, proving that if he was Prime Minister he'd have a beneficial effect on our country's young. Not so long back we decided to level the garden so that the kids could play basketball there. So we hired, on Sid's advice, one of those mini-diggers. Fantastic. The boys and I would get up early, have a nice bacon sandwich and a cup of tea, then spend the best part of three days controlling heavy machinery and doing what real men should do. The finished result was interesting, mind you, but no matter: the bonding process was complete.

But Sid's most enduring legacy would be the turnaround he would engender in marital relations in this country. If every man followed

Sid's lead, the instances of broken marriages would halve overnight. If a bloke found himself getting the seven-year itch, there would be no need for him to go out and find himself a mistress. In Sid's world, every man would love his drill. Solid, reliable, you don't have to buy it dresses or bring it flowers on Valentine's Day. It's always there when you need it, ready to do your bidding. And, as Sid told me, the ghost of a tear in his eye, a drill is always faithful.

Unless, of course, it's got a bit on the side.

Gordon Ramsay: prick with a fork

They say you should never meet your heroes. With that in mind, I hope I never meet Gordon Banks.

For those of you who don't know, Gordon was goalkeeper for my beloved Leicester City. Somewhat less significantly, he was part of the English World Cup side in 1966. And for the record, I should state that my desire never to meet him in no way stems from any worry that he would be anything other than a perfect gentleman. No, my problem is that I haven't had terribly good luck with Gordons in the past, and I'm beginning to think it might be a curse.

In my journalism days, I was one of the executives on the *News of the World*'s *Sunday* magazine. We had bought the serialisation rights to Gordon Ramsay's first ever cookbook, and all the sub-editors were moaning something rotten about how difficult it was to lay out, and how they didn't have enough time to do it. So, in a moment of misplaced enthusiasm, I decided to lay down the law. 'Right,' I announced. 'I've had enough of all this bloody moaning. I am going to lay out this week's extract.'

The recipe I had to deal with was for Gordon Ramsay's perfect soufflé, so I asked the picture desk for a few soufflé pictures, and some of Gordon in the kitchen, and I set to work. Well, I thought, as I started laying out the flat plans, this couldn't be more straightforward. What were all those whinging sub-editors moaning about? I merrily started writing captions, worked through all the ingredients and selected a picture to go above them – Gordon holding a bowl and whisking the egg whites for his soufflé to perfection. It can't have taken me more than half an hour, so off I popped for lunch.

It wasn't until several million copies of the magazine had been printed that I realised there was a little more to the sub-editor's art than I had previously thought. I opened up a copy to the pages I had devised, and there, perfectly placed, was my picture of Gordon whisking his soufflé. Unfortunately, the caption had inexplicably become mixed up with an instruction from the recipe: instead of reading 'Beat the egg whites until white and fluffy', or whatever it should have been, it read 'Prick with a fork'.

I understand that Gordon was less than pleased; personally, I was delighted to be holed up in a newspaper office, well away from the sharp end of his spatula.

To make a fool of oneself in front of one Gordon can be considered unfortunate; to make a fool in front of two starts to look like carelessness. Naturally, that's exactly what I did when I met Gordon Brown. I was asked by Channel 4's Jon Snow to do a sponsored walk around London for a cancer charity that was raising money for a special cancer unit at Charing Cross Hospital. The *Evening Standard*, for whom I write a column, was also backing the cause, so I decided that this was something

I really ought to do. I was also asked if I would help publicise the event by appearing in a photograph with Jon, the Patron and Gordon Brown – another supporter of the charity – at the Treasury. 'Sure,' I told the PR people. 'No problem. Happy to help.'

The night before the photo-shoot, I looked through the details I had been sent, and read a little note saying, 'Jon Snow and the Patron will be in walking kit.' I immediately started seeing the red mist and called the PR girl. 'Look,' I stormed, 'I should have been told about this. If I arrive dressed in a pair of jeans and a shirt I'm going to look bloody churlish and miserable, like I won't play along.'

'OK, Nick,' she replied in a calming tone of voice. 'What would you like me to do?'

'You've got to hire me the full gear. I want mountaineering boots, padded anorak, woolly hat, ropes around my shoulders, a mountaineering stick – you get the image. And make sure you get everything in extra large!'

Strop over.

The next morning, I arrived at the Treasury and met the PR girl. 'I've got it all, Nick,' she told me. 'In XL, like you asked.' It was a baking hot day, so I felt ever so slightly foolish dressing up as though I was setting out for a trip to one of the poles, but it was all in a good cause, I told myself. To make matters worse, there was increased security at the Treasury, and every time I went through a scanning machine it lit up like a Christmas tree thanks to all the paraphernalia I had attached to my person.

The upshot of all this was that I was the last person to arrive at the photo-shoot. Never mind, I consoled myself as I trotted down the corridor that led to the room in question, at least there's no doubt that I'll have the best costume. Preparing myself for gasps of admiration, I burst through the door. All I needed was a fanfare of trumpets – or perhaps more appropriately a chorus of yodellers – to complete my entrance.

And then I had one of those moments when I wished the ground would swallow me up.

Jon Snow and the Patron were standing by an attractive water feature making small talk with Gordon Brown. The full extent of their 'walking gear' consisted of a rather inconspicuous pair of walking boots around their necks.

They looked at me.

I looked at them.

A silence ensued that was so uncomfortable it would have had Harold Pinter feeling twitchy.

Ever the consummate politician, Gordon Brown broke the ice. 'Er, it's very good to see you,' he managed.

I struggled to reply, momentarily (and uncharacteristically lost for words). 'Thank you very much, Chancellor.' I strode forward, looking every bit like an extra from *Heidi*, and shook everybody's hands. I'm not sure whether they wanted to laugh or cry. 'I'll tell you what, Chancellor,' I babbled. 'Rather than betting on how quickly I complete the course, would you like to bet on whether I actually *manage* to complete it? On account of my size, and everything...'

Gordon looked at me with a slightly wild look in his eyes, clearly wondering how this demented nutcase had managed to get past security. 'We'll see about that,' he answered politely.

Typical politician. They never give you a straight answer...

London 2012? Let's have a Whopper and curly fries instead

Take a moment, if you will, to peruse the front cover of this book. You will observe, I have no doubt, that I do not have the frame of a gifted athlete – I have as much chance of taking part in the Olympics as Saddam Hussein has of winning the Nobel Peace Prize. There are rheumatic tortoises whose personal best at the 100 metres is better than mine, and beached whales that can manage a more impressive high jump. It doesn't stop me from liking sport. In fact I love it – my capacity for watching rugby is almost legendary – but I can't think of a bigger waste of time, money and jockstraps than bringing the Games to London.

The 2012 Olympics, we are told, will cost the average Londoner about the same as buying a Walnut Whip every week for the next ten years (that's about 38p for the Cadbury's Creme Egg eaters among you). Let's get this straight: if any government, local or central, tells you something like this, they're lying. Look at the Dartford Tunnel. They told us we would only have to pay to go through it for as long as they took to recoup their costs. We're still paying – and it costs a lot more now than a bar of chocolate. When they say it's going to cost as much as a Walnut Whip, you can bet your boots that what they really mean is a family-sized bumper Christmas tin of Quality Street – and they'll probably have removed all the toffee fingers as well.

We're told it's going to be fantastic, world class, a show of wonders the like of which we have never seen. But let's be honest – generally speaking, London couldn't hold a piss-up in Keith Floyd's back garden. Recently, a barge crashed into Battersea Bridge. This bridge has been spanning the Thames since Victorian times; it was bombed by the Luftwaffe; it is the last word in sturdiness. When it became clear that the repairs were going to cost somewhere in the region of seven figures, they started examining the possibility of banning the bridge to vehicular traffic. The city that reckons it can host the 2012 Olympics can't even keep a bloody bridge open that's been there since Victorian times.

It's great to have all this vaunting ambition for London, but we need to have it directed in the right way, to bring it home to the people who are stuck in traffic as they struggle their way home, to the people who live in fear of being mugged on the tube trains, to the people who haven't got enough buses or who are trying to cope with the problems in our hospitals. Instead of real solutions, they are being offered this fanciful sideshow of the 2012 Games to take their minds off the real problems of living in the capital.

And it's not just Londoners who have to pay for it – the whole country's going to be stung for the bill. Why? Why should people in Manchester pay? Why should people in Birmingham pay, or in Sunderland? The idea that they'll all be able to go and watch the games is absolute rubbish – they won't benefit from it any more than some eighty-five-year-old pensioner stuck in a council flat in Wembley will benefit.

But what about the feel-good factor? Supposedly the whole country 'felt good' after we won the 1966 World Cup. Productivity even went up, they tell us. But I don't buy it. We won the Ashes last year: it felt great, everyone (including me) was delighted, and we all went to work with a bit of a spring in our step. But don't try and tell me that the British public are so stupid, or shallow, or brain dead that they think to themselves, 'Hmmm... David Beckham has just scored the winning goal in the World Cup. I think I'll work harder at punching out these nuts or making these rivets or driving this bus.' It makes no sense. If anything, they're more likely to spend their time hanging round the coffee machine jawing about the match and the boss will have to give them a kick up the arse to get them to go back to work.

If, by any chance, some eleven-year-old kid is reading this and thinking to themselves, 'Right, I'm going to show that fat bastard and become the fastest runner in the world,' then that's fantastic and good luck to them. But the way I see it, if too many kids become obsessed with Olympic fever, it's going to be a terrible drain on our country's resources. Why? Because WE NEED FAT KIDS! We need fat children to keep McDonald's and Burger King and KFC in business. These places keep our school leavers in work! There's nothing else these poor buggers can do – they're so poorly educated (because we spend all our money on building Olympic stadiums and not science labs) that all they can do is serve hamburgers. And if we don't have any fat kids going to the burger bars, we'll have more people out of work, and our taxes will go up even more. They keep the very fabric of our fragile economy intact and to get rid of them is to risk complete fiscal ruin.

So let's give them a Walnut Whip and leave them to get on with it.

"I'll tell you anything you want – just don't make me use the step machine!"

The Spanish Inquisition: alive and well, and living in Holmes Place

So you thought the *Blair Witch Project* was scary? Well it's got nothing on my local gym – back in the days when I used to attend!

It's not the hellish instruments of torture on display that scare me the most, although I do admit that they are pretty terrifying. Frankly, these horrific machines, complete with steel tubing, weights, strings and pulleys, would have the chief torturers of the Spanish Inquisition rubbing their hands in glee, ecstatic that they've found new ways of inflicting the most horrible pain on their hapless victims. Their favourite would probably be that one that looks like an elaborate dentist's chair, but they'd no doubt put in a bulk order for those state-of-the-art rowing machines and they'd probably put themselves down for a few step machines, too.

Then there are the fitness instructors, of course. Anywhere else they would be the most frightening creatures imaginable – a sinister mixture of military commander and Bond villain – barking their excruciating instructions at their unfortunate prey, who seem unable to break out from under their spell, as though they were being controlled by some Jedi mind trick.

No, the most frightening sights any gymnasium has to offer must be the naked men wandering about in the changing rooms. They'll saunter out of the showers, using the little white towel that ought to be preserving their modesty to dry their hair with great vigour, then they'll put one foot up on the bench, smile an Action Man smile, and say, 'Hi!' in their manliest voice.

What sort of man is it that does this? Why do they think I would want to have a conversation with them before I've even put my jeans on? It's not as if we're all in the same rugby team or something, where we've been knocking around together for a few years and have got used to seeing each other in our birthday suits. No, this is some bloke that (a) I've never met before, (b) I'll never meet again, and (c) I never *want* to meet again because, frankly, having seen him *au naturel*, I'll never be able to look at him in the same way. (A case in point: when I did visit a gym for a short period of time, there was one bloke who was always doing this. I was fully prepared to put it all down to experience until one Saturday morning when I went into the local greengrocer's. Well, bugger me if it wasn't the same guy serving me with my fruit and veg. I couldn't make eye contact with him and I've never fully been able to enjoy parsnips ever since.)

Meanwhile, I'll sit there meekly trying to dry myself off with a similarly miniature towel, ruminating on Nick Ferrari's Universal Law of Naked Men. This states that the more naked a man gets in the gym changing rooms, the louder he becomes. So when he's wearing his pants and vest, he'll be loud, but just about bearable; as soon as he takes them off, he'll start talking like he's on a yacht in a Force Ten gale. I don't know why it is. Maybe they want everybody to have a look, although I'm reliably informed that it's the people with the least to display that display themselves the most (I'm unable to corroborate this, as I'm far too scared to look). I'm also told that this situation is not unique to the male changing rooms, but that there is a breed of female that gets up to the same sort of shenanigans. Strangely, I find that less offensive.

Of course, you don't just get strange men in the changing rooms. Most of these gyms now have exercise classes where you can pursue some means of inflicting pain on yourself under the misapprehension that you're actually enjoying it. I shan't shock you with a description of ordinary men taking part in an aerobics class, but I feel it is my public duty to reserve a word or two for the curious sight of grown adults practising martial arts. Somehow it would be alright if they lived on a Zen retreat in an obscure corner of Thailand, but I'm afraid I can't be doing with it in Penge.

Martial arts are OK if you're a kid. I grew up in a fairly sleepy Kentish village where not much really happened, so it was big excitement the day that one oriental inhabitant of the village decided to hold karate classes in the village hall. I was only about eleven or twelve and I had images in my head that I would be like David Carradine in *Kung Fu*. I would learn all these fantastic moves, which would serve me well when I found myself up against the bad guys who had tried to take a group of nuns hostage: I'd leap forward and with my newfound karate skills would be able to send guns flying, wrestle people to the ground and save the day.

Of course, it wasn't quite like that. We all queued up in our differing shapes, sizes and ages outside the village hall and were matched up with a partner of roughly our own build. In my case this was a rather hefty bloke who worked as a printer. His name was Dave. It was all a bit of a disappointment – Dave was no Scaramanga – but I was not to be put off and I threw myself into the lessons with gusto. I even passed a couple of exams and mastered the karate kick – somewhat to the chagrin of Dave the printer, as I managed to break his ankle in the process.

As I grew up, of course, the allure of karate lessons weakened. And you have to ask yourself why it is that grown men – indeed middle-aged men with kids of their own – feel the need to make fools of themselves pursuing this ridiculous activity. Don't believe them when they say it's a great form of exercise and discipline – so is sado-masochism, but you don't see them carting their leather whips and gimp masks down to Fitness First every Thursday night, do you? Or *do* you?

No, unless you are a member of the SAS, or the police force, or a crack anti-terrorist unit, or you really are likely to come up against a potential Scaramanga, I'm afraid that karate dads belong to a slightly suspect group of grown-ups, second only to boy scout leaders. (Quite why a grown man would want to run around in shorts, sleep in the woods, look after a group of smelly children, eat baked beans out of the tin and sing songs about goolies round a camp fire is beyond me. Personally I'd prefer a stint in Belmarsh.)

So there you have it: instruments of torture; slightly damp, naked men; karate dads with a screw loose. I know, I really should do some more exercise, but is it any wonder I can't muster the enthusiasm?

That's enough touchy-feely — let's bring back the nasty party

I've got a confession to make. A guilty secret. Just between you and me, OK?

When I was a lad, no more than seventeen, I ran for office. To tie in with the general election, our school held an election of their own and I was selected as one of the political leaders my fellow students were to vote for. So far so innocent. But here comes the really bad bit: I ran for Labour.

My policies were a vote-winning mix of Michael Foot and Billy Bunter: Russia's great, America's evil; benefits for all; state ownership of everything; bigger portions at lunch; and more chips. Needless to say, I was voted in with a landslide majority.

They say that if you're not a socialist at twenty you haven't got a heart and if you're still a socialist at forty then you haven't got a head. I think it has something to do with property ownership. When you get your first flat, you become a conservative with a small 'c'; when you sell that flat a few years later and buy yourself a house with the profit and see the way the market can work for you, you become a Conservative with a big 'C'. Personally I was ahead of my time – I managed to get all that left-wing nonsense out of my head before I even left school.

The two questions I get asked most since I started my radio show are (1) How did you ever get that job in the first place? and (2) Why don't you go into politics? My answers are always, respectively, beats me and I'm tempted. Not so long ago I had the Mayor of London on the show and a woman phoned in to say, 'You know, Mr Livingstone, you're always going to get in unless Nick Ferrari runs, because he's the only person who could beat you.'

'Mmm...' replied the mayor, 'I'd welcome that. It would be fun.' Ever the diplomat – I can imagine what he was really thinking...

The truth is that, while it would be intriguing to go into politics, I'd only seriously consider it if I could be fabulously and flagrantly corrupt. It's not so much that the money isn't good – the mayor gets a pretty decent salary – but that all the opportunities for a bit of a bung from various builders and developers and hotel groups and whatever would be far too tempting. I'd only really be interested in the job if I could say, 'Look, I've been given this really fabulous set of golf clubs and life membership of the Belfry. As a result we're going to build a Holiday Inn right in the middle of the City. It does mean we're going to have to pave over the River Thames, but it's all in a good course ... I mean cause...'

As that seems unlikely to happen, I think I'll just stick to what I do best: tending towards being a natural Conservative and Thatcherite, and banging the drum for that.

The Conservative Party used to be referred to as the natural party for government. They were a patrician and a paternalistic crowd – especially some of the classic Tories of the glory years, like Willie Whitelaw – and they came into politics with a genuine belief that they had a mission to serve and that they could make the country a better place. They were a party of strong convictions. They've lost all that now because the brilliance that is the marketing of New Labour has meant that that whole area of politics has disappeared and there is now only this centre-ground politics: the left has come over and taken most of the right's good clothes.

So what are we left with? The Conservative Party is arguably in its biggest state of disarray since it was started in 1834 as a result of the Tamworth Manifesto. For a start, they get through leaders quicker than I change my socks. We have several annual events to look forward to nowadays: Wimbledon, the Grand National, David Blunkett being forced out of the government in disgrace, and the election of a new Conservative leader. What nobody seems to understand is that we need to go back to the good old days of Tory politics: decrease tax for the rich, increase selective education and the number of grammar schools. If you're doing quite well, or have aspirations to do quite well, we should be rewarding you. If you are a lazy, backsliding, scrounging skiver who expects to live off benefits, we should be coming at you with bared teeth and making life positively tough.

As you may now be aware, I am of the opinion that Conservatives shouldn't do touchy-feely. There seems to be this ridiculous fear in the party at the moment that they are perceived as the 'nasty' party. Well that's not true – they're actually perceived as the unelectable party – but when they *were* perceived as the nasty party they were actually a bloody successful party. They had seventeen years in power and established an incredible economic platform that saw us through all the way until 2004. You don't have to be nice and touchy-feely to achieve things in life. Look at Alex Ferguson – he's achieved incredible successes in the field of sport, but he's no pussy cat. And you can bet your bottom dollar that if Chelsea walk into the dressing room 3–0 down to Bolton Wanderers, Jose Mourinho won't be sitting down there thinking, Now what I really need to do is be touchy-feely and explain to them where they're going wrong so that they have the opportunity to better themselves in the future. He's going to give them a good kick in the unmentionables and send them out to turn the game around. Why do you suppose Tesco is so successful? Their executives don't sit around saying, 'Yes, we need to be all lovey dovey and make sure our workers all have a jolly nice day.' They say, 'Right, we're going to kick the crap out of Sainsbury's.'

The same is true of politics – indeed, it's even truer, because politicians so often have to make such difficult decisions. You don't have to go out of your way to be nasty – you don't wake up in the morning and think, Hmmm... How can I grind down a few more single mothers in Brent today? – but politics is tough and running a country is tough, so you've got to be tough if you want to do it...

Which, of course, begs the question: what *do* you do with those single mothers living in Brent? Well, if they have already fallen into the poverty trap, clearly you have to offer them some degree of benefit. But then, once they are back on their feet, if they continue not to work, you stop those benefits. It's as simple as that. It is vital that we encourage people to discover the joy of work, which is an absolute liberation. And it has a double hit: not only does it stop people claiming benefits, it will stop people going to the NHS to be treated for depression.

It might sound trite, but it's obviously true. The most important thing in life is to look after your family; the second most important thing is to empower yourself by getting some work and earning yourself a bit of cash. So we have to say to single mothers and others who find themselves caught in the benefits trap, don't just troop down to the dole office every Thursday afternoon in those bloody sweatpants you've been knocking about the house in for the last four days, your three kids in tow all guzzling Sunny Delight. Go and get a bloody job. You'll feel fantastic about yourself and guess what: if you work hard, and this is the amazing thing, you'll get money. It will be money that you've earned, there to spend on what you want. Instead of sitting there on your ever-expanding backside, you've gone out and done a day's work. Now that's empowerment.

Unfortunately, these self-evident truths appear to have been lost in the blanket of ridiculous touchy-feely Conservatism. This is especially galling for natural Conservatives such as myself, because it is compounded with the fact that we have in Tony Blair the best Conservative leader this country will never have. There was a key point in his evolution as a young man when he did not quite know which way to jump politically. Then a crucial thing happened: he met Cherie. She was obviously left-leaning because of her background (her father, the actor Tony Booth, was a famous Labour supporter) and so that was the path he decided to follow. It was a disaster for the Conservatives, because Blair could have been the natural successor to Margaret Thatcher. Even now you can't help feeling that he is a Tory wolf in the sheep's clothing of New Labour.

But as you get older, you get a little wiser. In my case, you also get a little fatter. And as the inches gather and the grey hair arrives and everything ceases to be quite in the position it should be, you start to realise that, actually, all politicians make promises they don't keep. No matter what end of the political spectrum they come from, there is not much any of them can do about the issues that affect our lives: there is always too much crime on the streets, tax is always too high, you're always concerned about your children's safety and you could always do with an extra few bob in the bank. No political party that's ever come along has really made any profound difference to that and none ever will. So while I mourn the passing of true Conservatism, I'm not going to lose any sleep over it. And that's why, corruption aside, you won't find me on the hustings for the next Conservative party leadership vote, which should be in, ooh, about six months, shouldn't it?

"It's a jar of pickled onions... but with Damien's signature on I reckon we'll clear 40 or 50K."

Dead cows and white elephants

'What's that, Michelangelo?'
'What's what, your Holiness?'
'That.'
'That's the creation of Adam, your Holiness.'
'Right.'
'Don't you like it?'
'Um…'
'I thought you wanted the ceiling decorated to the greater glory of God with images that illustrate His everlasting greatness.'

'Well, yeah, but it's a bit, er, traditional, isn't it?'

'What do you mean?'

'Well, I was thinking along the lines of something more conceptual.'

'Conceptual?'

'Yeah. I thought we could have half a cow suspended from the rafters. And maybe the artist's unmade bed sitting in front of the altar. I mean, this painting's alright, but wouldn't it be a bit more contemporary if we rollered over it with hint of magnolia and then spattered some horse shit on it?'

What an excellent thing it is that Damien Hirst and Tracy Emin weren't born 500 years earlier. Who knows – a conversation like that might just have happened!

Call me a fuddy-duddy – I'll probably take it as a compliment anyway – but my idea of art is one of fabulous landscapes and paintings and sculptures that truly take one's breath away with their beauty and the skill of their execution. I don't think I'm alone in believing that the cobblers we're force-fed under the guise of modern art really is just the most preposterous rip-off.

But do you know what? That's fine. So long as wealthy private investors want to fund this kind of art, so be it. Look at Charles Saatchi. All credit to him – he's a classic example of the success of commercialism, he's a gifted bloke, he's made a big pile of money out of his advertising agency and if wants to spend hundreds of thousands of pounds buying unmade beds and deck chairs, good luck to him. I think he's bonkers, but good luck to him. And he's clearly on to something I don't quite understand – he made millions out of selling a pickled shark by Damien Hirst that he had bought for a snip at fifty grand.

Where it becomes very different is when the meddling hand of the government gets involved. They see the publicity that this nonsense attracts and they can't resist showing off how hip and trendy they are to all their friends in the Islington set and how firmly they have their finger on the pulse. And so we arrive at a ridiculous situation whereby £70,000 is paid for an enormous piece of stone to be installed at the entrance to a London hospital. The idiotic arguments for doing this are numerous: hospitals are public places, so they should be prime locations for public art; many people have their first encounter with art in hospitals, so it has an educational value; it is even claimed that the existence of this lump of stone makes healthcare staff more relaxed and efficient.

Of course, all these arguments ignore the one

important point: that £70,000 spent on a big rock is £70,000 not spent on making people better. And as for the argument that it improves the welfare and efficiency of hospital staff, what complete baloney. They'd much rather have somewhere where they can go and have a fag (the percentage of health workers who smoke is astonishing...) rather than standing outside in the pissing rain trying to keep their cigarettes alight. That would improve their day, not a big stone. It is quite clearly a flagrant and ghastly abuse of public money. I don't believe you would find a single worn-out junior doctor or a nurse living on a wage so minuscule that they can't even buy themselves a small flat, who would consider that £70,000 on a stone is a good use of public money.

Of course, this waste of public money is not restricted to modern art. Consider this fact: the biggest single advertiser across all media in this country is the government. It is spending our money advertising to us. And what is a huge chunk of this advertising money spent on? Making sure we get all the benefits we are entitled to. So we find ourselves in a situation whereby, as if we're not been fleeced enough by these people who never do a day's work and live off benefits, those of us who do actually work and pay our taxes give our money to make sure these lazy buggers pick up every last penny they are entitled to. It's a kick in the teeth for every hardworking taxpayer in the country.

What is most galling about this shameful misuse of our money is the fact that our politicians seem to do it with such disregard for our opinions. We can always have our say at the polls, they inform us self-righteously. If I've heard one senior politician tell me this on the radio show, I've heard a hundred but, of course, we have to wait up to four years for the next chance to have our say. Most people can't remember what they did last Thursday, let alone remember another example of the ever-increasing catalogue of misuse that we seem to be presented with. So it's left to people like me – broadcasters, writers and commentators – to keep these travesties fresh in people's brains. So here goes: remember the lunacy of the Millennium Dome? Don't buy this nonsense that seems to be peddled around that it was a great success story. It was an absolute, unmitigated disaster, the biggest white elephant this country has ever seen. And it displays perfectly the fact that this wasteful profligacy with our money is common to all politicians – it was started by a Conservative Prime Minister and endorsed and completed by a Labour Prime Minister. It would almost be funny how much of a pig's ear was made out of the whole project, if it were not for one thing. The Millennium Dome cost £800 million – the equivalent of 16,000 pickled sharks. Think how that could have been spent in the fields of health, education and law and order.

Suddenly it doesn't seem so funny any more, does it?

Order, order! Why some honourable members need some real whipping into shape

There is a weekly treat in the business of politics that I try to savour as often as I can. It is called Prime Minister's Question Time.

If the Prime Minister is asked a question by one of his own party, you can bet that it will be along the following lines: 'Will the Prime Minister agree with me that the latest government initiative to improve street lamps in my own home village of Lesser Swelling has been nothing but an unqualified success?' To which the Prime Minister will answer, 'Thank you very much, and I would like to take this opportunity to inform the house that we intend to extend this scheme to the rest of the country.' There will be much cheering from his side of the house.

If a member of the opposition asks a question, it will be more in the following mould: 'Will the Prime Minister agree with me that he is nothing but an ill-informed oaf with a frankly ridiculous haircut and a suit that fits him like a sack of potatoes, and that he should be escorted forthwith to the Tower, placed in the stocks and pelted on a daily basis with rotten eggs and rancid tomatoes?' There will be much baying from one side of the house and cheering from the other. And so the ancient process of our parliamentary democracy continues.

Given half a chance, I too would like to pose a question at Prime Minister's Question Time, and this would be it: 'Does the Prime Minister agree that the current crop of politicians should be fired immediately on the basis that the political scandals they are providing to us, the electorate, are simply not good enough.'

It is often commented on that we don't vote enough in elections and it is true that the British public seems not to be terribly engaged with modern politics. Part of that is to do with the fact that we are all living a comfortable life and we don't think that politics really affects us; a significant part of it, however, is down to the fact that our politicians are simply not working hard enough to grab our attention with their scandalous behaviour.

Of course, it wasn't always like that. Back in the glory days of the Conservative party, politicians really put their back into it, earning their keep with a succession of scandals that kept us entertained every time we opened our Sunday newspapers. No longer are we treated to the image of a Conservative minister's wife standing at the gate of the constituency house in the country, surrounded by her two or three lovely children, one of them still in her Wellington boots having been shipped in at the last minute from the local gymkhana. The wife would be holding a tray of tea and chocolate digestives and giving a fabulously insincere statement to the press in a slightly wobbly voice: 'I'll stand by him. He's the man I love. This was just an indiscretion.' Yes, the Tories truly were the Chelsea of political scandals (indeed Chelsea played a part in one of them – who can forget the wonderful image of David Mellor getting up to his nefarious activities in the football strip of his favourite team).

In deference to those lost days, I have taken the liberty of compiling my top five political scandals. I hope you enjoy this nostalgic trip down memory lane.

In at number five is the gloriously greasy Neil Hamilton. The murky intricacies of the suggestion that he accepted big brown paper bags of cash in order to table questions in the House of Commons kept us entertained through a large part of the 1990s. With a good scandal, the devil is in the detail: somehow it would simply not have been juicy enough if he had accepted his bungs by electronic transfer. The brown paper bags showed his desire to abuse his public position had real spirit: he truly was a master of sleaze.

A close fourth is Jonathan Aitken. Had his scandal simply encompassed a few freebies in a posh hotel and a whisper of involvement in a dodgy arms deal it would scarcely be worth mentioning – such things are par for the course for any 1990s Tory politician worth their salt – but he makes my list thanks to the chutzpah with which he defended himself even against the most hopelessly incriminating evidence. Anyone who can claim that he will use 'the simple sword of truth and the trusty shield of fair play', and then end up behind bars a few months later, is clearly a true master of the sleaze merchant's art.

A shock entry at number three: John Major. For years we thought that the most exciting thing that happened to the former Prime Minister was when Norma forgot to put butter on his peas; then, out of the blue, we learn that Maastricht wasn't his only contentious affair when he was in power. Again, he might not have made the list had the object of his desires been some bubbly blonde bimbo. His greatness lies in having a crack at the last person in the political world we would have expected anybody to make a beeline for – Edwina Currie! – and for providing comedians with a rich source of 'I'm going for a late-night curry' gags henceforth.

Finding himself just short of the number-one spot, but without question worthy of a gong, is the redoubtable Jeffrey Archer. His fall from grace has all the hubris of a Greek tragedy, though thankfully none of the grizzly murders. How we drooled when he successfully sued a newspaper for half a million quid for suggesting he had engaged the services of a lady of the night. How we laughed when a crusty old judge said of his wife, 'Has she not grace? Has she not fragrance?' How we rubbed our hands with glee when, several years later, having appeared to have got away with it, his alibi fell to bits and he found himself sentenced to four years for perjury. You couldn't make it up – a yarn too improbable for even one of his novels. Thank you, Jeffrey, for your services to sleaze.

But victorious in the number-one spot is the granddaddy of scandals, the original and still the best: Profumo. What more could you want? Call girls, the Minister of War, Russian spies, members of the Royal Family and libidinous weekends at fantastic country estates. The Profumo scandal ticked all the boxes and threatened to tip the country into widespread anarchy. That's the way to do it.

So the Tories, as in so many other fields of endeavour, really knew how to handle themselves when it came to scandal and sleaze. They encompassed it all: cash, sex, intrigue, perjury and prison. But what do we have nowadays?

David Blunkett.

He's the very best candidate New Labour can field against the Tory giants. So let's have a look at his indiscretions. He appropriated public money to buy his girlfriend a train ticket to Sheffield. And he bought some shares.

Runner-up in the New Labour sleaze rankings has to go to Peter Mandelson, I suppose, but his qualifications are equally unimpressive: he helped a couple of blokes get a passport and he lied to the bank about his mortgage. Hold the front page!

No, these people just aren't trying hard enough. They really need to consider what it is we pay them for and how they are going to gain the country's acceptance. If I were a political leader, I know exactly what I would do: I'd go out and recruit Premiership footballers and soap stars to high-profile ministerial positions, people who could be guaranteed to go out, get drunk and end up with their trousers round their ankles on a regular basis. It's the only way to get politics in this country back on track.

Did you hear the one about the Pope and The Most Holy Carmelite Order of Prestatyn?

Pity the poor journalist.

I know that journalists don't necessarily spring to mind when one considers the people in the world most deserving of your pity, but having door-stepped with the best of them, I know perhaps better than anyone the trials and tribulations that the search for, er, truth can inflict upon the humble tabloid hack. Allow me to share a few of them with you.

The Pope was in town. This was quite a big deal and the press coverage was huge. I had just washed up on the *Sunday Mirror* as a reporter. If you're on a Sunday paper, Saturday is your big day, the day when you are effectively a news reporter (as opposed to the other days when you spend your time digging up mucky stories about all and sundry). On this particular Saturday, his holiness had an especially busy day, starting with an address to a crowd of monks and nuns in Richmond Park at five in the morning. I was assigned to cover the event and was very happy to do so – I would be thirty feet away from this remarkable man and it would be a moment I would remember for the rest of my life.

And it certainly was, but for very different reasons.

What I didn't count on was the fact that it was the photographer's fortieth birthday the night before and he was celebrating it at a tiny hotel in Richmond. The sensible thing for me to have done would have been to go to bed early with a good book (or at the very least with somebody who had read one) and prepare myself for the early-morning encounter with his holiness. I should have groomed myself spiritually to be in the presence of God's representative on earth.

Needless to say, this is precisely what I didn't do. An extremely merry time was had by all and

I ended up rolling into bed at three in the morning. When the alarm went at four, I could barely bring myself to cover my eyes to ease my headache, let alone cover the Pope's address to his faithful servants. I tried to make myself look vaguely respectable, cursing as I did so that Nick Ferrari's Law of Shaving Cuts dictated that this would be quite impossible. (This law states that the more important the engagement, the deeper your shaving cut will be. Working on the radio has made me a bit lazy – nobody can see you, so you can go four or five days without shaving and it doesn't really matter. But I like to make an effort when I'm on the television. Given that I'm nearly always going to be taking a pretty controversial point of view, the least I can do is make sure people don't think, What a great, fat, scruffy, unshaven git with all those horrible views. Much better that they think of me as a great, fat, scruffy, *cleanly shaven* git with horrible views and superb hair thanks to Nicky Clarke and teeth courtesy of Dr Wyman Chan of Smile Studios. But Nick Ferrari's Law of Shaving Cuts dictates that the more high-profile the show, the more likely I am to turn up with my cheeks looking like I've had a face massage from

Freddie Kruger. And as a man who has had more shaving cuts than he can count, let me warn you against the snake-oil merchants who tell you of miraculous cures for them. As a young man I was assured that pouring pepper on the cut works wonders. Not true. It gives you a sensation not unlike, I imagine, sliding down a razor blade into a bucket of aftershave; and what's more you have pepper on your face, which looks very silly indeed...)

Dishevelled, hungover, bleeding and no doubt exuding a fragrance not unreminiscent of a barrel of Old Peculier, I somehow managed to haul myself over to the park and the Pope.

By the time I arrived, feeling distinctly wobbly, there were already thousands of monks and nuns there. I did my best to fight my way through them and get to the press area, but by the time I had managed to do so, the Holy Father was just about finishing; before I had a chance to write down even a single word, he had switched off the microphone and everyone started leaving.

I knew that the news editor would have my guts for garters if I was unable to file anything, so I called the office and read out my story to the copytaker. Even as I was reciting it I knew it was unacceptably feeble. Half an hour later, as the area was all but empty, I called in again to check what they thought of the story. The news editor comes on the line. 'Hello, Nick.'

'Hello.'

'Look, Nick, with the greatest of respect...' I always worry when someone says that. Nick Ferrari's Law of Offensive Comments dictates that any sentence starting with 'with the greatest of respect' is likely to be the most disrespectful thing you've ever heard. 'With the greatest of respect, this is a load of unmitigated crap. We were watching it all on the television and you haven't caught any of it.'

'Right,' I replied sheepishly.

'Look, there are some sisters there who have come out of their convents for the first time in forty years to see the Pope. It's the first time they've seen the world as we know it today, the first time they've been allowed out. Talk to them. Find out what it's like seeing Britain for the first time since the war. See what they think about cars and buses and trains and fashion. You've got Sweet FA here.'

'OK,' I say, looking around to see the coach

park practically deserted and neither hide nor hair of a nun. What I did see was one bloke with a clipboard and a yellow jacket, so I approached him. 'That coach that just left,' I ask him. 'Was it full of nuns?'

'Yes, it was, actually.'

'Great. Who were they?'

He looks down at his clipboard. 'They were from The Most Holy Carmelite Order of Prestatyn.'

'Great,' I tell him, writing this down, 'fantastic. Thank you.' Time to make some quick decisions. Clearly I'm not going to be able to interview a nun as they'll all be halfway up the A3 by now. But hey, I think to myself, nuns aren't likely to read the *Sunday Mirror*. And if they do, they're certainly not going to sue. So, pen and notebook in hand, I decide to let my creative juices flow. '"It was like the world had opened before my eyes," said Sister Margarita of The Most Holy Carmelite Order of Prestatyn. "I saw the Holy Father, but I also saw the liveliness and the excitement of the modern world. I had forgotten the vibrancy, the colours and the imagery." Sister Teresa agreed with her. "I never thought the world was like this," she told me.

"The Holy Father has opened my eyes."'

This, I tell myself, is fantastic stuff. Pure poetry. OK, so there's a bit of artistic licence going on, but nobody will be able to tell that. So I call the copytaker and file my new story.

Half an hour later I call back again. 'Hang on,' says a voice at the end of the phone, 'the news editor wants a word with you.' Now, this is not normally good news and I'm kept waiting for several minutes to find out what he wants to say to me. Finally he comes on the line. 'Right, Nick,' he says. 'I've got the copy.'

'Good.'

'So this is from The Most Holy Carmelite Order of Prestatyn, is it?'

'That's right,' I bluff.

'And you got all these quotes, did you?'

'Absolutely.'

'Good. Well done.'

'Thank you.' I breathe out a sigh of relief.

'It's all the more impressive,' the news editor adds, 'given that The Most Holy Carmelite nuns of Prestatyn are a silent order.'

A little silence of our own ensues.

'Now then, Nick, would you like to revisit this story.'

'You know what,' I splutter. 'I think I probably do.'

Not all the sticky situations I found myself in as a journalist were entirely of my own making. Another memorable one occurred when I was working on the *Sun*. In those days, the *Sun* was never happier than when it was having a good bit of argy-bargy with somebody. If that somebody was from another country, so much the better. We regularly had a go at the Germans over the beach towels and, as a *Sun* reporter, I even led my own invasion of Germany accompanied by a couple of Page 3 girls, the comedian Stan Boardman and two army Jeeps. However, my finest moment in battle occurred when I was chosen to spearhead the *Sun*'s invasion of France to protest against the French farmers who were burning our English lamb at the time. Calais had once, many years ago, belonged to the British, so the editor decided that the time had come to take it back.

I was not alone in my mission. In fact I had sterling back-up. There was another reporter, three photographers, a Radio 1 DJ, the town crier of Hastings, a butcher and a Princess Diana lookalike. As if that weren't a motley enough crew, we were all in fancy dress. The other reporter went as a Beefeater; the Page 3 girls were dressed in skimpy bikinis with *Sun* logos; the three photographers were let off; the Radio 1 DJ went as a lance corporal out of the 3rd Duke of Norfolk Highlanders; we couldn't get the town crier out of his bloody suit, nor stop him from ringing his bell and shouting 'Hear ye! Hear ye!'; the butcher had a stripy apron; and the Princess Diana lookalike was dressed as, well, Princess Diana – only in a rather kinky, very short skirt. I was dressed as a good old British bobby.

You can imagine the looks as we all traipsed off the hovercraft and through customs. Most of them, of course, were directed at the leggy, half-naked Page 3 girls, but I managed to turn a few eyes (and no doubt several stomachs) myself. The French, as is their wont, failed to see the funny side of it and the first thing they did was to arrest me. It was, I had not realised, illegal in France to enter the country in the uniform of another nation's police force without prior consent. As Jean-Paul and Pierre led me off to the detention room to start their cross-examination for my heinous crime, I turned and shouted out selflessly to my comrades in arms, 'Keep going! The invasion must continue without me!'

Eventually I managed to sweet-talk my way out of this unfortunate predicament and catch up with my unit. The scene was extraordinary. The butcher was handing out lamb chops to some very confused passers-by; the Page 3 girls were stalwartly attracting the attention of various French gentleman, despite the fact that it was cold enough to freeze the proverbials off a brass monkey; and the kinky Princess Diana was eliciting some most peculiar stares indeed. We may not have regained Calais, but we certainly made our mark.

On the way back, the crossing was so choppy that the other reporter had to be sick into the tin hat of the lance corporal from the 3rd Duke of Norfolk's Highlanders: an inauspicious end to one of the oddest days of my life...